'Preachers, Bible students, and lovers of the gospel will find that Sam Gordon has once again done us all proud. *Magnificently researched and attractively illustrated, this page-turner of a commentary pulsates with the very life that puts new vigour into churches everywhere.'*

Richard Bewes OBE,
Former Rector, All Souls Church, Langham Place, London

'This commentary combines careful attention to the text with a contemporary flavour. It reads like an up-to-date account of how God works in the lives of people today. Great for those who teach and for personal devotions.'

Erwin Lutzer,
Former Senior Pastor, The Moody Church, Chicago, IL

'Sam Gordon has given the student of the Bible a fine in-depth study on 1 Thessalonians. This book will exceed your expectations in what to expect from a verse-by-verse study.'

Charles Stanley, Senior Pastor, First Baptist Church, Atlanta, GA, President and Founder, In Touch Ministries

5 MARKS

OF A

GOSPEL
CHURCH

1 THESSALONIANS
MADE SIMPLE

Shalom!

SC

2 Cor. 4v7!

5 MARKS OF A GOSPEL CHURCH

1 THESSALONIANS MADE SIMPLE

SAM GORDON

40 Beansburn, Kilmarnock, Scotland

5 MARKS OF A GOSPEL CHURCH

© 2018 Sam Gordon

ISBN-13: 978 1 912522 43 9

Cover design & typeset by Pete Barnsley (CreativeHoot.com)

Printed by Bell & Bain Ltd, Glasgow

DEDICATION

to

the *Truth for Today* Accountability Board
with immense gratitude

Esther, John, Peter, Ruth, and Wallace
pilgrims together on the journey

check out the Truth for Today website
www.truthfortoday.co.uk

FIRST WORD

Gospel is a third millennium buzzword!

Many of you will be familiar with gospel partnerships where a group of like-minded local churches join forces for evangelism and mutual encouragement (where I live, for example, we have the Yorkshire Gospel Partnership). We talk freely and openly about gospel-hearted people, gospel leaders, gospel principles, gospel passion, and gospel initiatives; we warmly embrace gospel ministry when it is firmly anchored to Scripture and we take our hats off to those whose sacrificial service is driven by their unashamed commitment to the gospel of Christ (Romans 1:16).

We are passionate for church members to live their daily lives in a manner that is gospel-centred and gospel-focused. In today's wishy-washy world of evangelicalism, our ministry mindset and theological nous are best shaped when the gospel is our default position. Across the pond in the USA we have the highly-acclaimed organisation, The Gospel Coalition, and a biennial conference appropriately called T4G (Together for the Gospel).

We even refer to some local congregations of God's redeemed people as gospel churches because they clearly display signs of gospel integrity. Such a label could be tagged onto the church in Thessalonica.

Given that scenario, the important questions are: What makes a church, a gospel church? What defines it? What is its hallmark? What is its DNA? The answer to those questions, and more, is found in this Pauline epistle!

Sam Gordon

CONTENTS

Mark #1

A church where faith is flourishing

There was something exceptional about the believers in Thessalonica. They stood out! Different. Distinctive. Distinguished. None of your average, run-of-the-mill, one-size-fits-all, plain vanilla bores in this church. These guys and gals were not content to just keep the engine ticking over. They were Holy Spirit-powered, gospel-driven, and faith-fuelled. Dynamic, enthusiastic, and so avidly keen. On the ball.

These first-century pilgrims were excellent role models of authentic, biblical Christianity. They were committed to gospel-drenched justification. The real McCoy! Paul even describes them corporately as the ideal church. That is, a church with the right stuff. A gospel church. A good and godly church. A church in a city where Paul caused a riot. A church that 'turned the world upside down' in order for it to be right side up

(Acts 17:6). That says something. It had not always been like that!

Before Paul arrived in town on one of his famous, highly publicised missionary journeys, there was no church there. The reality is it was through his sterling evangelistic efforts that a gospel church was born.

First things first

Let me take you back for a moment to Acts 17 to where and when it all began. This chapter is compulsive reading. Good stuff. God stuff. Riveting. A fast-moving account of all that transpired in those early days. The big question is: What actually happened?

- Paul preaches his heart out about Jesus Christ.
- Scores of people are gloriously converted.
- The locals do not like what they see and hear.
- Rent-a-mob is activated and the devil fights back.
- There is pandemonium as chaos and confusion reign supreme.
- Paul and Silas come out of hiding and do a vanishing act in the middle of the night.
- They turn up in Berea, forty miles down the road, and preach the same message to a better class of people.
- Wonder of wonders, history almost repeats itself.

Thumbnail sketch

Thessalonica was quite a city: a place of renown; a city

with a reputation. It was originally named Therma from the many hot springs adjacent to it. Then in 315 BC it was renamed by Cassander, one of the top officers in the army of Alexander the Great. He called it Thessalonica because he wished to dedicate the city to a lady of that name, the half-sister of Alexander the Great.

During the next century Rome became the dominant power in the region and Macedonia was absorbed into the expanding Roman Empire. History informs us that in the early decades of the first century BC the security of the Roman state was seriously threatened by civil war. Competing generals fought to control what was then the Roman Republic.

During those turbulent years the ordinary peoples of the Empire looked on rather anxiously from the sidelines, bemused and concerned as they wondered which of the rivals would come out on top. As far as Thessalonica was concerned they had no need to worry, the outcome could not have been better.

She made a wise choice and sided with the eventual victor, Augustus; with victory in the bag he became the first Roman emperor. This loyalty was amply rewarded when Thessalonica was made the capital of the province of Macedonia. It was also awarded the status of a free city and enjoyed the benefits of self-government under locally appointed rulers. In fact, Lightfoot described it as 'the key to the whole of Macedonia' and then he added that 'it narrowly escaped being made the capital of the world.' So important was the city that one of the writers of that time,

Meletius, once said, 'So long as nature does not change, Thessalonica will remain wealthy and fortunate.'

Location, location, location

As a city it occupied a strategic position for it boasted a splendid natural harbour, a substantial harbour, at the head of the Thermaic Gulf (now the Gulf of Saloniki). It was situated on the *Via Egnatia*, the main route between Rome and the Orient. The Arch of Galerius which spanned the Egnatian Way in Paul's day still stands today.

It proved to be a thriving centre for trade and commerce, as goods from east and west poured into the city. The shops and markets were well stocked with all sorts of consumer products: you name it, they had it; and if they did not have it, they could get it for you!

Thessalonica had the ambience of a fashionable luxury resort with so much going for it. In terms of real estate its location was enviable. First impressions would take your breath away. It has been called the crown jewel of Macedonia. Its setting is picturesque with the majestic mountains of Greece, including the fabled Mount Olympus, rising high behind it. Its economy was stable. There was an air of affluence permeating the atmosphere of the leafy streets of the city, which in its own way contributed to the considerable influence of her well-to-do citizens.

Headcount

In Paul's day the population was conservatively estimated to be around 200,000 souls, and rapidly rising. The city and its environs attracted a potpourri of people who came from all over the world to settle there, making it a truly cosmopolitan centre. It was the New York, Houston, or Boston of its day – yet, as Mark Howell comments, 'for all its assets, Thessalonica was a lost city…. a pervasive spiritual darkness covered [it].'

During World War I the city served as an exceptionally important Allied base. Then in World War II the city was captured by the advancing German army and the Jewish population of about 60,000 persons was deported, never to be seen or heard of again.

It is possible to visit Thessaloniki (aka Salonica or Salonika) in Northern Greece as part of a package holiday deal. I was there a while back when involved in some Bible-teaching ministry across the border in Macedonia. Apart from any seasonal adjustment brought about by tourism, the population hovers around the one million mark, making it a big, bustling city, second in size only to Athens. Some of Greece's most creative musicians including Savopoulos, Tsitsanis, and Papazoglou came from this city which is renowned as the cradle of modern Greek popular song, Rembetiko (the Greek Blues). It is also the birthplace of Greek basketball. A huge honour was bestowed on the city when it was chosen in 1997 as the cultural capital of Europe.

Head start

It was into this situation, two millennia ago, that Paul ventured on his second missionary journey. As a trailblazer and visionary for the gospel, he saw it as a potential springboard for evangelising the rest of Europe. How right he was, as subsequent events indicate! How did he go about it? He went to where the people were when he made a beeline for the local synagogue. And when he got there he started where the people were. In his preaching he assumed they knew nothing. He led them through, step by step, into a clear understanding of the great truths of the gospel.

We learn a lot from Paul's direct approach to evangelism: he used the word of God and he declared the Son of God. There were two main points in his sermon: Jesus died and the Lord has risen. An inexpressibly powerful message! There were no slick programmes, no bags of tricks, and no eye-catching gimmicks to influence others. On the contrary, it was the Holy Spirit applying the word of God to extremely needy hearts. What a marvellous response. Tremendous!

Paul simply sowed the seed; it was watered by tears in the place of prayer; then God came, and in his sovereign goodness, the Lord gave the increase. A significant number said 'yes' to Jesus Christ for the first time in their lives.

Bringing in the sheaves

Actually, there is a trio of fascinating phrases employed by Dr Luke to focus attention on the wide range of new converts. He says that 'some of [the Jews] were persuaded … as [were] a great many of the devout Greeks and not a few of the leading women' (Acts 17:4). We know the names of a couple of them, Aristarchus and Secundus (Acts 20:4). Put them all together and these folk became the nucleus of the first gospel community in this metropolitan city.

When we touch base, it is all about proclaiming the story of the Lord Jesus and then seeing people come to know him in a personal way. There is the sheer joy of evangelism, it is reaping a harvest of lives dramatically changed by the power of God. These are the ones who would turn the world topsy-turvy because they had been transformed from the inside out. They did not leave their world the same way they found it!

How to give away your faith

Paul's time in Thessalonica was relatively brief, but it was hugely significant. I imagine he and his companions would have stayed there a while longer if circumstances had been more favourable. However, Paul being Paul, he made the most of his time by maximising every opportunity afforded to him. He did not mess around with other people's lives! Sure, the message of the cross never changed, it was the presentation that differed on occasion.

It is instructive to note that four phrases are used by the historian in Acts 17:2-3 to underline the tactics that Paul adopted:

- 'he reasoned with them from the Scriptures' –
  he engaged in some form of dialogue, a kind of
  question and answer session; in so doing, he did
  not talk *about* the Scriptures, he reasoned *from* the
  Scriptures

- 'he explained' – he opened up the word of God

to them by exercising an expository ministry; he wanted them to know what was said and where the Scriptures said it

- 'he proved' – he presented all the evidence to them clearly and distinctly

- 'he proclaimed' – as he preached the word, he was making a bold declaration of biblical truth

Class 101

Having watched them come to a personal faith in the living God, Paul begins to carefully disciple them. He excelled in the art of nurturing, where no stone was left unturned and nothing was too much trouble. He invested his energy and experience into ensuring they got off to a good start in their Christian lives. He covered an awful lot of ground in the space of a few short weeks.

The lasting impression we have is that here was a group of gospel people grounded in the fundamentals of the faith, enthusiastically keen in their quest to know the Lord better, and immensely grateful to Paul for his ministry among them. They were big-hearted and generous in giving their money to the Lord's work, shining brightly for their Lord in a pagan environment, and passionate in their desire to engage in evangelism.

Knee-deep in Greece

Time marches on and with it inevitable and unavoidable changes come. Paul himself has moved on. He is redeployed to a city that tops the league in terms of sinfulness – the Vanity Fair of ancient Greece – Corinth, aptly described as a sailor's favourite port, a prodigal's paradise, a policeman's nightmare, and a preacher's graveyard.

Even though the apostle finds himself knee-deep in Greece, in a situation which is less than user-friendly, there are many thoughts flitting around in his mind as he reflects on the infant church in Thessalonica. How would they cope, he keeps asking himself. Will they manage without him being around any longer, he wonders. Do they have the theological know-how and get-up-and-go to stand on their own two feet?

Typically of Paul, he does not wait to find out. He takes the initiative, seizes the moment, strikes while the iron is hot, and sends them a letter. Paul wrote his first epistle to them around AD 50/51. It is from Corinth that his amanuensis puts quill to parchment in a valiant attempt to encourage and reassure them. Basically, the legendary Paul wants to remind them of his continued interest in them and his prayerful concern for them. He knows how he feels about them, but he has to communicate that message to them, for they need to know it as well. It was not the classic case of out of sight, out of mind. If anything, the opposite is more accurate. How could he forget them? They are family, his spiritual sons and daughters. They matter to him because they are important to God.

A first-century stimulant

What makes this I-can't-get-you-out-of-my-mind letter so

appealing and attractive? Paul writes to pep up people who are struggling, for whom the future appears ominous. He emboldens them. He does it in a way that is unforgettable and unique. He is generous with his encouragement – a kind of verbal sunshine, it costs nothing, it warms hearts, and enriches lives. The best time to give a bouquet of flowers to people is when they are alive, not when they are dead.

It is special because in every chapter he talks about the second coming of Jesus Christ, the 'blessed hope' of the child of God (Titus 2:13). There is no finer incentive to living a life of holiness and no better spur to motivate us for gospel ministry. If we really take to heart what Paul is saying and believe it with a no-strings-attached commitment, then it will lead to a deepening of our spiritual lives. We shall never be the same again.

Paul never looked on the imminent return of Christ as a theory to be discussed by armchair cynics waiting for the end of the world. He saw it as a truth to be lived in the humps and hollows of everyday experience. It is a clarion call to readiness, a wake-up call to live today in light of tomorrow.

Lessons to learn

- God uses homespun people – he did not send a celebrity angel to go and evangelise Thessalonica; he sent a converted Jewish rabbi and a couple of his upwardly mobile friends.

- There is power in the gospel – it did not take years to plant a church in this great city. God's power was enormously effective in changing lives and a viable church was up and running in less than a month.

- Satan still opposes the proclamation and advance of the gospel, and he continues to ruthlessly persecute the people of God. When Jesus is faithfully preached, you do not have to go looking for trouble; trouble will often come looking for you.

1:1

One-to-one

Paul gives us a fascinating, behind-the-scenes look at an evangelical congregation who met together in the middle years of the first century AD. And what an eye-opener it proves to be! His letter is no more than a heart-to-heart talk to his children in the faith. It is a fairly compact epistle, packed full with parental affection and advice.

Here was an ideal church, one not given to extremes at either end of the spectrum. They maintained their spiritual glow, they sounded out the message of redemption, they were waiting with a sense of expectancy in their hearts for the second advent of Jesus, there was a clearly defined balance in their walk with God – those hugely positive thoughts permeate the first chapter.

Sweet and sour

Did you know that the church has a fragrance? Paul referred to it as a 'sweet aroma'. This is what Eugene Peterson said in

2 Corinthians 2:14-15 in *The Message*, 'In Christ, God leads us from place to place in one perpetual victory parade. Through us, he brings knowledge of Christ. Everywhere we go, people breathe in the exquisite fragrance. Because of Christ, we give off a sweet scent rising to God, which is recognised by those on the way of salvation, an aroma redolent with life.'

In the past few years the putrefying stench of sin has invaded some high-profile ministries thereby obscuring the fragrance of Christ. If we give the media an inch they will take a mile as they callously exploit every whiff of scandal. They jump on the bandwagon and before we know it they have blown the whole picture out of proportion. When that happens, the man in the street, who cannot see the wood for the trees, writes the church off as a non-starter. Our reputation is dealt such a ginormous blow that we end up severely winded. The body of Christ then becomes a punchbag for cynics eager to poke fun. Postmodern man turns up his nose at the church. Such is life in the third millennium.

To be fair, that is only part of the story, it is not the total picture. The truth is, there are many more ambrosial churches than there are rotten ones. There are many flowers that are both delectably fragrant and deliciously fruitful. When I flick through the pages of the New Testament, and I come across a gospel church like the one in Thessalonica, I quickly realise there are some pristine lilies in a muddy pond.

They certainly had a reputation, a good one. Thank God, it was for all the right reasons!

Let me introduce ...

How does the apostle start the ball rolling? What are his opening comments? Is there anything that grabs our immediate attention? I think there is! The introduction! Pithy. Short and sweet. Straight to the point.

The intro begins with a single word, *Paul*. He signed off the epistle. He was, in the words of Charles Haddon Spurgeon (1834-92), 'the prince of preachers'. As an emissary to the regions beyond, he took the gospel where man had never taken it before. Paul, a flagship missionary, sailed the world with the story of Jesus. He held major citywide crusades and planted scores of churches all over the place. He was a prolific writer in huge demand across Europe, Asia, and the Middle East as a Bible teacher. Paul's vision for mission was as big as the world he knew. Unlike many of us, he was not guilty of dreaming too small. He knew he served a great God who could do great things through him if he placed his life at his disposal.

It is always fascinating and not a little intriguing to observe how a person introduces himself, for it tells us something about them. It is, therefore, most refreshing to read, in light of his stellar credentials, that Paul did not introduce himself as an apostle; he was content just to say, 'Hi, I'm Paul!' In spite of a colossally impressive résumé, plus a long list of unbelievable achievements in his illustrious career to date, he makes no attempt to enhance his own image. He does not need to, he does not have to. He is comfortable with himself and is most relaxed with a passing reference to his name.

He is plain Mr Paul. What staggering, make-your-head-swim humility! There is a magnificence in his sense of insignificance. This man is a Titan, but he is also a man with a servant heart. Dwight Lyman Moody (1837-99) remarked that 'the measure of a man is not how many servants he has, but how many men he serves.' True service begins where gratitude and applause end. Servanthood is basin theology (John 13:1-17). Whose feet are you washing?

Once seen, never forgotten

One ancient writer actually described Paul in this way, 'He was a man small of stature, with a bald head and crooked legs, in a good state of body, with eyebrows meeting, and nose somewhat crooked.' Well, when we read that, I suppose we could say, once seen, never forgotten! If we met him downtown in the shopping mall we would not look, we would stare! However, what Paul might have lacked in good looks, he more than made up for in being a willing, tireless servant of the living God.

George Whitefield (1714-70), hailed as 'the apostle of the English Empire' by his contemporary Augustus Toplady, mightily used by God in the First Great Awakening, had a squint. The Welsh evangelist, Christmas Evans (1766-1838), had a false eye. Twenty minutes into his sermon his eye socket would fill up with moisture. He would pause, take out the false eye, wipe the socket with a handkerchief, and pop it back in again!

Paul, a robust preacher, stands unique in the annals of church history as one who combined the animated fervour of an evangelist-cum-church planter with the gentle tenderness of a shepherd, the skilled diplomacy of an ambassador, and the astute intellect of a scholar.

Team ministry

Paul is not ploughing a lonely furrow, for he also includes *Silvanus and Timothy* in his cordial greetings to the church. They were his co-labourers. Silas (or Silvanus, a Roman name meaning 'woodland') was a highly esteemed member of the Jerusalem congregation. He was one of the 'leading men among the brothers' (Acts 15:22) and was credited with having a prophetic gift. Unlike some people, he was happy to play second fiddle. On the other side of the preacher, Timothy (which means 'honouring God') was Paul's son in the faith. He was relatively young, in his late teens or early twenties, sensitive by nature, fairly raw and inexperienced. When it came to gospel ministry, he was still in the process of cutting his teeth.

Even though the three men are individuals in their own right, they combine well to form a brilliant team ministry. Each one has a distinct role to play ensuring their spiritual gifts are used to their full potential. When Billy Graham received his Congressional Medal of Honour, the first thing he is reported to have said upon receiving the award is, 'This has been a team effort from the very beginning.' He then proceeded to name the people who had ministered alongside him through the years. In closing, he said, 'We did this together.'

From Paul's perspective, he is enormously grateful to the Lord for his colleagues as people. He values them for who they are and he treasures their genial fellowship. He recognises their superb contribution to the ministry and is big enough in heart to acknowledge it. Paul does not feel threatened by their gifts. This is not a one-man show; he is not into empire-building. All that matters to him is that the kingdom of God is extended. He is not convinced of his personal indispensability. He knows he is just one of a trio who make up the team and who need each other's support and input.

As a servant, Paul is more than willing to reduce his own impact so as to enhance theirs. A competitive spirit and the scourge of professional jealousy have no place in his heart. He is the kind of person who does not mind who gets the credit so long as the job gets done! O yes, we can be too big for God to use, but we can never be too small!

Best of both worlds

Paul addresses his epistle to *the church of the Thessalonians in God the Father and the Lord Jesus Christ*. A double address. One tells me where we are geographically, the other where we are spiritually. Two places at once, they were here and there at the same time. Our hearts are in heaven, our feet are on Planet Earth. God's church was living in Thessalonica and their church was living in God. To be sure, the preposition *in* has a different nuance in these statements, since the church is *in God* as the source from which its life comes, whereas it is *in* the world only as the sphere in which it lives. Having said that, it is correct to say that every church has two homes, two environments, two habitats: it lives in God and it lives in the world!

When Dale Ralph Davis was Professor of Old Testament at Reformed Theological Seminary (Jackson, MS), he used to sign his notes, 'In Christ in Jackson.' That was how he conceived of himself – 'That's who I am,' he would say, 'I'm in Christ in Jackson. Jackson is where the Lord has me and I'm in Christ.' That is precisely what Paul is saying to the believers in Thessalonica!

The apostle wrote numerous epistles during the course of his ministry, but this one is unmatched. It is the only letter that employs the phrase *the church of.* They were a company of called-out believers enjoying a remarkable sense of unity in their midst. There was a discernible bond, a wonderful feeling of affinity, a rich spirit of togetherness throughout the congregation. It was palpable. There was a beautiful atmosphere that could be felt the minute one went through the front door and entered the meeting room. Electric. Spine-tingling. What a church!

'In' the know

There is a lot more to it than meets the eye. There always is! These guys had no background. It was not a case of sporting the 'been there, done that' tee shirt for they had no core of experienced members in the congregation. They were a motley crew of still-in-the-diaper Christians, freshly converted from Judaism or polytheistic paganism. This God stuff was all brand new to them. They have only been going for a few months, at most. Raw recruits. Christian rookies. In a world where men wobbled like Jello, their convictions have been recently acquired. In a permissive, *dolce vita* society their moral standards have been newly adopted. The nagging question is: When tough times come, how would they handle a crisis? This helps explain why Paul said what he did in his tête-à-tête, for they were rooted in God, living in God, and secure in God. The dynamic relationship they enjoyed with the Lord was such that it was extraordinarily close. They were *in him*. In other words, they share in his life. They may be green behind the ears, but make no mistake about it, God was totally committed to them.

Double-barrelled blessing

It was the norm in Paul's day that whoever wrote a letter signed their name at the beginning rather than at the end! It was also a convention of first-century correspondence to include a prayer for the recipients at the outset. *Grace to you and peace* is the twofold blessing he offers them, the twin towers of the gospel. Paul could not have wished anything better for them because, as Alistair Begg notes, 'The grace of God introduces us to the forgiveness of sins, and in that, there is peace.'

Grace and *peace* are two of the loveliest words in a believer's vocabulary. They sparkle like lights on an evergreen Christmas tree. There is a certain pizzazz about them, a vivacious dash of divine wonder. They are not rights to which we are entitled, they are gifts that are given to the church.

The order is important. We can never know peace in our hearts without first experiencing the grace of God in our lives. Peace is a wonderful spin-off from the grace of God. If we look at it from a different slant, grace is the fountain of which peace is the stream. Grace is God's multiplex kindness in our lives. Grace is something that comes to us which we do not deserve and which we cannot repay. Grace stoops to where we are and lifts us to where we ought to be. John Pantry hit the right note when he penned:

Wonderful grace
That gives what I don't deserve,
Pays me what Christ has earned,
Then lets me go free.
Wonderful grace
That gives me the time to change,
Washes away the stains
That once covered me.

Peace happens within us; it is a freedom from inner distraction, an internal rest, a feeling of well-being. Spiritual wholeness. It is a tranquillity of soul that frees us from fear and takes the sharp edges off our anxiety. It is that unruffled quietness which defies the crashing, crushing circumstances of life.

- peace with God
- peace with ourselves
- peace with our partner

- peace with our neighbours
- peace with our past
- peace with our present
- peace with our future

A terrific greeting! A great, big, wonderful God!

Chilling with God

This God of grace and peace who came to their church in the first century to meet their miscellaneous needs is the same God who comes to us, two millennia later, saying, 'Put your trust in me.' Paul's sanguine letter speaks as powerfully today as it did then. God's grace overflowed in their hearts and his peace reigned in their lives. Pure and simple, that is the prime reason why their marque of Christianity was so infectious and exciting.

Before we take a look at the rare qualities exemplified in the church at Thessalonica, it would be helpful to spend a moment with the apostle himself.

1:2

Then sings my soul

What made Paul tick? His mindset is described and it is abundantly clear that there are three important facets to his life. There is praise! It is fairly obvious, even to a casual observer, that Paul was a man with a song in his heart. Even when he found himself in a prison cell, he quickly turned it into a place where he could celebrate the goodness of God.

We read all about that earth-moving incident in Acts 16:22-34. He preached about praise, wrote about it, and practised it. Praise did not change his situation, but it radically transformed his attitude and gave him a new outlook on life. Praise does not come easily when we find ourselves in hot water. In trying circumstances it is not the most natural thing to do. We make the choice to do it, or not do it. It is an orientation problem that needs to be conquered.

Another dimension is added when we realise that praise is often referred to as a sacrifice (Hebrews 13:15). Where we have sacrifice, there is always a price to pay. It costs. It is not a light-hearted singalong led by someone with an overdose of charisma acting as cheerleader. In fact, praise has nothing to do with ambience or a man's personality; it has everything to do with Jesus and our relationship with him.

Thanks!

So what does Paul do? We read, *we give thanks to God always for all of you.* That is a felt expression from a profoundly grateful heart, a note of glad appreciation. It is when we consciously say 'thank you' because we see it as a debt we owe. How that must have perked them up. Paul writes and tells them that he feels the way he does about them, the horizontal component. His delirious praise is directed heavenward, the vertical vector. They would be uplifted and God would be exalted.

I am sure that boosted their flagging morale and really blessed them. He turns to them and says, 'Thanks for the privilege of being with you.' Then he turns to God and says, 'Thanks, Lord, for letting me be there.' How easy it is to pray for people who give us every reason to be grateful. Generally, they prove to be accepting and affirming, real instead of phoney, supportive and giving rather than subversive and grabby. They gave Paul a host of reasons to be thankful. We should also give people reason to be thankful to the Lord for our presence and input in their lives.

There was a personal touch to his praise. He strikes a similarly rich vein when he writes letters to other churches, especially Romans, Ephesians, and Colossians. There is a practical element to it as well. Do you recall what he said about Philemon as an occasion for praise? He spoke warmly of his love for all the saints and how he refreshed the hearts of the saints (4-7).

Looking at it from another standpoint leads us to see this spirit of thankfulness as a partnership. For example, in Philippians it is associated with their fellowship in the gospel (1:3-5); when writing 1 Corinthians, the emphasis is on the provision of God's gifts to them (1:4-9); in his second letter to the same church, he reflects on the fact that God's mercy reached down to him (1:3-11). More often than not it is linked with people, and we see this in his words in 2 Timothy when he remembers with fond affection his younger colleague (1:3-7). The highlight of this praise mingled with thanks is probably found in Galatians where the apostle is meditating on the death of Christ (1:3-17).

Praiseathon

Praise is an essential ingredient in the life of any Christian. I wonder, how often did Paul do it? It was *always*. See that? Paul was no fool, he was not born yesterday. He was not naïve and his head was not in the clouds. He knew there were problems, difficult people to handle, tensions that arose from time to time, and clashes of personality. But, in spite of all their hang-ups and shortcomings, he thanks God for each one.

Pray on, brother

The second great influence in Paul's life is prayer. He is the kind of man whose praise is coupled with prayer. The emphasis here is on their fellowship in prayer. He uses the phrase *in our prayers* which implies the three of them met together as a leadership team to seek God's face for the church. A prayer triplet. Meet for breakfast, meet for prayer!

How essentially important it is for those in responsible positions in gospel ministry to take time out to pray. Prayer is the slender nerve that moves the muscle of omnipotence. Down on our knees is where burdens are shared, battles are fought, and victories are won. It was standard practice when they met together. They did not think or talk about it, they did it!

To many of us, prayer is about as exciting as changing a punctured tyre on a narrow country lane. To Paul and his ministry colleagues, time spent in prayer was never seen as wasted time. It is astoundingly profitable, paying handsome dividends. It is quite remarkable to realise that a year down the road these folk are still lovingly upheld at the throne of grace. They remain on his prayer list. He genuinely cared for them by praying for them.

A prayer list, a prayer diary, a prayer card are useful tools that enable us to tap the potential of heaven on behalf of one another. If we use an app like PrayerMate on our smartphone, or write a name down, or stick a photo on the fridge, we are less likely to forget to intercede for that person. Paul thanks God for them and he talks to God about them.

1:3

A people person

The third vital factor in Paul's life is people. Paul was not on an ego trip, nor was he immersed in himself in his own tiny world. Far from it! This man deeply cared for others. People mattered to him. He had an expansive heart. We could never say that Paul was selfish or self-centred, his attitude is above and beyond reproach.

When his eyes scanned the congregation as they gathered for worship in the urban sprawl of Thessalonica, he sincerely thanks God for them. Not only a few of them, or the ones who were easy to get along with, but every single one of them. This kind of love is not confined to those we like, nor is it restricted to those who like us or those we would like to have like us. There is nothing selective about it because Paul is not enmeshed with the clique mentality. That takes some doing!

No church is perfect and they were no different from those anywhere else. Flesh and blood. Fallible specks of humanness with good and bad points. In spite of their prosaic ordinariness, they were saved by God's outrageous grace and were an unfeigned joy to his heart. In a spiritual sense, Paul fathered and mothered them, for each conversion under his ministry was like the birth of a baby. And each new church was like a nursery, full of the joys and challenges of new life. Because of this nonpareil relationship, he saw beyond the externals and saw Christ in them. And because he prayed for them, he was able to thank God for them. He loved them for the sake of Jesus.

Rhapsody

We see the authentic effusiveness of his commendation as he writes about those who mean so much to him. There is bona fide warmth in all he says. He is concerned about them; they weigh heavily on his mind. Like any doting father on the move, his heart ached for his bairns back home. Paul wanted to be with them so much, but that was just not possible! He wanted to make sure they were getting their proper spiritual nourishment, to protect them from lurking strangers like the Judaisers who were determined to lead them astray, to soothe and allay their fears, to guide them through difficult decisions, and to prepare them as best he could for the future, for he could see the storm clouds gathering on the horizon.

All these matters are going through his mind and, as if he did not have enough on his plate, they were all there at the same time! So, in the course of his opening remarks, he thinks about them a minute or two longer. He knows there is so much he could say, but he pulls up the reins and narrows it down to three tremendous attributes. These ace qualities underline the humongous blessing this gospel fellowship has enjoyed and experienced. It is no wonder they are an inspiring group to be with.

Creative faith

This is what Paul means by the phrase, *your work of faith.* He is not speaking about the initial act of saving faith at the moment of their conversion. The faith outlined here is a faith that is active, a faith that works, a faith that performs, a faith that produces fruit. True faith is not sterile. Faith that does not act is not faith at all. Faith for them was not a wall plaque or a car-window sticker; it was a life-changing encounter with Jesus Christ. Such was their unflinching confidence in God, their total commitment to Christ, and their out-and-out reliance on the Holy Spirit that things were really happening in their church.

- faith to move tall mountains of obstruction and difficulty

- faith to venture out into an antagonistic environment in courageous witness

- faith to believe God for miracles

- faith to see that a cup of ice-cold water given in his name matters in the great scheme of things

Holding the umbrella

Their faith was ingeniously creative and they had something to show for it at the end of the day. The story is told of a rural community which was experiencing a severe drought. Farmers watched helplessly as the corn crop shrivelled under the unrelenting sun. The ground cracked and dust devils swirled through the fields. Weeks passed with scarcely a cloud in the sky. As concern deepened into panic, the church that served the community declared a day of prayer to ask God for relief from the drought. The appointed day arrived and the community came to the church to pray. Farmers and men dressed in dungarees sat beside bankers and businessmen as the town united in asking God for rain.

One young girl walked into the church clutching an umbrella. 'Why are you carrying an umbrella?' some school friends asked in jest. 'Well, we are praying for rain!' responded the girl. She had taken to heart the motto of the Boy Scouts: Be prepared! She had faith. Simple faith. Childlike faith. Faith that was willing to trust God implicitly. Faith that believed God could do and would do what he was being asked to do.

Redemptive love

The word used by Paul is important, for we need to realise that 'labour' is different from 'work'. He pays fulsome tribute to their *labour of love*. The thought is of hard toil. It is energy expended to the point of exhaustion. There was a weariness in the ministry which they felt as they broke through the pain barrier and their strength was spent. Drained.

What prompted them to do it? Love! Love that was prepared to sweat, travail, and sacrifice. Such love can only be interpreted in the light of Calvary – a love that will pay anything, give anything, and do anything for the sake of the gospel. A love that counts all but loss, for making known the message. Love is the driving force, the propelling thrust, the motivating factor. Why? Because love always finds a way. This is an exquisite quality that sets believers apart as the children of God. This love is not abstract, misty-eyed, and insubstantial, but tough and practical. It works wonders, for God's love truly changes everything.

It is not an *ichthus* fish sign dangling pendulously from the neck or a gilded silver dove decorously impaled upon the lapel. These are mere symbols of our faith. The birthmark of the Christian is love. The most powerful, four-letter word in the English language is LOVE.

Aggressive hope

Paul puts it eloquently when he speaks of their *steadfastness of hope in our Lord Jesus Christ*. Alistair Begg concurs when he writes that 'our salvation is characterised by hope; it's one of the distinguishing features of the believer.' Let me tell you what it is not before I tell you what it is! It is definitely not the grin-and-bear-it mentality, nor is it the smile-and-shrug-your-shoulders syndrome. It is not the phlegmatic resignation of a Stoic with a grit-your-teeth-and-get-on-with-it attitude. It has absolutely nothing to do with offhand speculation but everything to do with resolute confidence. Triumphant fortitude. Stickability. Dogged determination. It is hangin' in there because you are hangin' on to the Lord! It is like the kettle, up to its neck in hot water, but it keeps on singing! It is the bounce-back factor.

When they were under enormous pressure, and they were; when they were living in abject poverty, and they were; when they experienced sore persecution, and they did – they endured. No matter what life threw at them or kicked in their teeth, they were resilient and showed a cheerful spirit. As William Barclay so aptly puts it, 'A man can endure anything as long as he has hope, for then he is walking not to the night, but to the dawn.'

What inspired them? Why did they not call it quits? Why did they not throw the towel into the ring? What kept them plodding on? Hope! Hope that it would quickly end, no! Hope that it would soon go away, no! Hope in the promised return of Jesus, yes! They were looking ahead and planning for the future. They were operating with their eyes trained on the distant horizon. They scanned the skyline and lived their lives in the future tense. They felt something was in the offing, but did not know when.

The eminent physicist, Michael Faraday, made no secret of his personal faith in Jesus Christ. While he lay dying, he was chided with the question, 'Where are your speculations now, Michael?' 'Speculations?' he retorted, 'I'm dealing in certainties.' So he was! So are we! They had:

- A faith alive – it was resting on the past as they looked back to a crucified Saviour.

- A love aglow – it was working in the present as they looked up to a crowned Saviour.

- A hope aflame – it was aiming for the future as they looked to a coming Saviour.

'True faith's work is never wasted, real love's labour is never lost, hope's resilience is never disappointed,' writes Philip Greenslade. Real Christianity is not benign. Someone said a church is made up of two kinds of people, the pillars who hold it up and the caterpillars who crawl in and out each week.

Improving your serve

The way a person works is very revealing. Working because of faith makes a humble worker; in other words, we acknowledge that the Lord is the only one who can give the increase to our labours. Love makes an industrious worker since our motivation is our grateful love for the Lord Jesus. We recognise that it is his work, not ours. Hope makes a persevering worker since we know that one day we shall reap a harvest if we faithfully sow the seed and do not lose heart.

When we put them all together – faith, hope, and love – they are like three legs of a stool, they need to be kept strong and balanced. You see, Christianity is not a work to be endured for duty's sake, it is a person to be served for love's sake. That explains why this fellowship in Northern

Greece was a pastor's delight, a shepherd's dream. An exciting bunch of gospel people in a gospel church! Surely that is the reason behind Paul's ability to say, 'Thank you, Lord. There's no people in all the world like your people.'

1:4

Past, present, future

Paul reminds the young believers in Thessalonica of three great facts in the opening chapter when he shows them where they have come from, where they now are, and where they are going. The turning point came as a direct result of the truth expounded in this verse, *For we know, brothers loved by God, that he has chosen you.* In layman's language, we can be saved and know it.

This is the immovable ground of our assurance, the bedrock of our salvation, and the unbeatable proof that we belong to Jesus. It means the ebony darkness can be dispelled, the pesky doubts can be dismissed, and the tricky devil can be defeated. A gargantuan fact. An incredible statement that is so incredible, it is jaw-dropping.

God's worldwide family

The opening two phrases help us grasp the all-out wonder of our relationship with each other in the global family of God. They also magnify the mystery of God's involvement in our lives. There is a word of assurance for Paul says, *for we know.* There are no doubts, no ifs, no maybes, and no buts. These few words ooze with solid certainty.

Then there is a sense of affinity for the apostle identifies them and is happy to call them, *brothers*. This would indicate they were all members of the same worldwide family. He looked upon them as his spiritual brothers and sisters.

Inside track

What does Paul know? What is he aware of? What is he convinced of? *That he has chosen you.* This sublime doctrine is the cornerstone of our faith for it ensures that God gets all the glory for his work of grace in our hearts. A great sinner who embraces a great Saviour always finds a great salvation. When Paul took one look at the saints in Thessalonica, he saw the quality of their life in Christ and the fruit of the Holy Spirit in their lives, and that is when he sensed in the depths of his own heart that they really are the people of God.

- God called them.
- God chose them.
- God claimed them.

In other words, they are elect! Simple as that! Well, is it? The moment we mention election, some people are frightened and begin to panic, others are confused, still more are thrilled with the sheer wonder of it all and joyfully declare, 'It's a smash hit!'

Be circumspect

So what do we do when we find ourselves caught in the

middle between two opposite feelings, between a rock and a hard place? I realise we are walking through a potential spiritual minefield, but we shall pick our steps carefully. We cannot pass by on the other side and pretend it is not there, it is! It is in the chapter, it is in Scripture, and we cannot skirt around it.

We must grasp the nettle with both hands and ask the question: What does the phrase *he has chosen you* mean? Warren Wiersbe has wisely observed, 'Try to explain it and you may lose your mind, try to explain it away and you may lose your soul.' We may never plumb its unfathomable depths for it is beyond our comprehension this side of heaven. Understand it? Never! There again, do you understand how a brown cow can eat green grass and give white milk and yellow butter? We enjoy the products! I cannot explain it, but I can enjoy it.

C H Spurgeon was once asked how he reconciled God's election with man's responsibility to make a choice. Apparently, the great London preacher answered like this, 'I never have to reconcile friends.' It emphasises the wonderful grace of Jesus and I am thrilled about that. It leaves me gasping for breath. I often feel like the psalmist in moments like these; I just want to stand in awe and wonder and shout at the top of my voice, 'This is the Lord's doing; it is marvellous in our eyes' (Psalm 118:23). Rejoice!

- We are chosen *in* Christ.
- We are chosen *by* Christ.
- We are chosen *for* Christ.

There, in our being chosen, is the mystery of the grace of God, the marvel of the love of God, and the miracle of the salvation of God. We should be satisfied to declare with the anonymous poet:

I sought the Lord,
And afterwards I knew,
He moved my soul to seek him,
Seeking me.
It was not that I found,
O Saviour true,
No, I was found by thee.

- So far as God the Father is concerned, I was saved when he chose me in Christ before the world began (2 Timothy 1:9).

- So far as God the Son is concerned, I was saved when he died for me at Calvary (Galatians 2:20).

- So far as God the Holy Spirit is concerned, I was saved on Sunday 11 February 1968 in Bangor, Co. Down (Titus 3:5).

The wonder of it all

Over the years, during the course of pastoral ministry, it was my delight and privilege to share in quite a number of wedding services. On the odd occasion, and thankfully, it has not been too often, I had the misfortune of hearing a stage whispered comment, 'What did she ever see in him?'

I sometimes think, when I see the Lord in his impeccable beauty that I may be tempted to ask myself the question, 'What did he ever see in me?' The unsurpassed pleasure of it all causes me to reflect on the words penned by James Grindlay Small (1817-88):

I've found a friend, O such a friend,
He loved me ere I knew him,
He drew me with the cords of love,
And thus he bound me to him,
And round my heart still closely twine,
Those ties which nought can sever,
For I am his, and he is mine,
For ever and for ever.

That is what happened to the Christians in Thessalonica. But it was not a first-century wonder, nor was it a spectacular phenomenon restricted to the halcyon days of the early church. Certainly not! For two thousand years later, in your life and mine, if we know Jesus, the same has happened! I do not know what that does for you, I know what it does for me, and I just want to pause, take a deep breath, and say, 'Thank you, Lord.' When your head spins with the mystery of election, let your heart also swell with the reality of grace.

1:5

You got it, you pass it on

Paul sees the church as a community of ordinary people who receive and transmit the gospel. It was fairly natural for him to move on in his mind from God's church to God's gospel because he could not think of either without the other. The plain fact is, it is by the gospel that the church exists and it is by the church that the gospel spreads. Each depends on the other, each serves the other!

In verses 5-8, the apostle outlines in three clear stages the conspicuous progress of the gospel in Thessalonica:

- stage one: *'our gospel came to you'* (verse 5)
- stage two: *'you received the word'* (verse 6)
- stage three: *'the word of the Lord sounded forth from you'* (verse 8)

Paul says it came to you, you received it, and you passed it on! This sequence is God's continuing purpose throughout the world! We unpack what Paul is saying by looking at what he writes here, *Because our gospel came to you not only in word, but also in power and in the Holy Spirit and with full conviction. You know what kind of men we proved to be among you for your sake.*

The first word *because* is a link word. Paul does that a lot! He wants to keep their attention. It joins what has gone immediately before with all that follows after. It automatically connects all that he said in verse 4 with what he is about to say in verse 5. Paul says, 'I know you are numbered in the elect; I know you are loved by God; I know you are among the chosen of the Lord.'

How did Paul know? How could he be so sure in his own mind? Here is the only reasonable explanation: when the gospel was preached and the good news of Jesus proclaimed, something inconceivable happened. And it only happened because the 'gospel is the power of God for salvation to everyone who believes' (Romans 1:16). Spurgeon said, 'The preaching of Christ is the whip that flogs the devil; it is a thunderbolt, the sound of which makes all hell shake.'

Talking the talk

When the truth of God was declared to them, it came *not only in word, but also in power*. The gospel did not come to them with words only, but it did come to them with words! Words matter. Words are important. They can be a scalpel or a sledgehammer depending on who wields them! They are the essential building blocks of sentences, by which we effectively communicate with one another. And the gospel, as we all know, has specific content which is why it must be articulated and verbalised.

In our evangelism, whether upfront or behind the scenes, we need to take the trouble with our choice of words. Most of us probably realise that words on their own are seldom enough, they may be disregarded or misunderstood; because of that they need, somehow, to be enforced. That is why words spoken in human weakness need to be confirmed with divine power. In all our gospel ministry, we need God to come and do what he does best.

This potency is not dependent upon our natural ability or know-how, it has nothing to do with man's eloquence. A man may have the gift of the gab, he may have kissed (or swallowed) Ireland's famous Blarney Stone, but that is not enough. It is the work of God's Spirit that gives authority and authenticity to that which is promulgated.

Why did the psalmist prefer to be a doorkeeper in the house of the Lord? So he could stay outside while the sermon was preached?! Some preachers do not need more fire in their sermons, they need to put more sermons in the fire! True power, a divine anointing – unction in our gumption – will bring glory to God, rather than to a particular individual. This brand of power is not worked up, it is prayed down. It is not always visible, but it is promised. This serves to highlight the powerful nature of Scripture. Explosive. What Semtex plastic gelignite is to the terrorist, the word of God is to the sinner. Dynamite! No matter when or where the gospel is broadcast, God is actively working.

Lights on

The message also comes *in the Holy Spirit*. Only the Spirit of God can illumine a darkened mind and quicken an enslaved will. We desperately need God to work, and when he does he uses the medium of his Holy Spirit. Therein lies the secret to effective gospel ministry and productive preaching. We must never divorce what God has married, namely his word and his Spirit. The word of God is the Spirit's sword (Ephesians 6:17). John Stott notes that 'the Spirit without the word is weaponless and the word without the Spirit is powerless.'

It came to them *with full conviction*. It was decisive. Paul's evangelistic preaching was not only compellingly influential in its effect, it was confident in its presentation. He was 'as sure as eggs is eggs' of its message, its truth, and its relevance. He believed it! In consequence, he was bold in trumpeting it.

There was impassioned conviction in the heart and voice of the preacher, and there was old-time conviction in the hearts and minds of those who listened. When this man preached he looked for signs following; he expected results, and he was not disappointed! Hearts were opened, deaf ears unstopped, and scales fell off their eyes.

These pagans were transformed into new men. They came from the realm of inky-black darkness into a totally new world of light and they emerged from the tomb of death to walk in newness of life. In a split second, they became a redeemed community. They proved the gospel actually works.

The figures speak for themselves

Paul's parting shot in verse 5 makes it clear that he is not making claims that could not be substantiated: his track record speaks for itself. This is terrific, for that is how Paul knew they were a chosen people! And, wonder of wonders, the same is true of us. So far as I am concerned, I have not the faintest idea who the company of the elect are, that is why I continue to preach the gospel of redeeming love at every possible opportunity. And when in the goodness of God some dear people respond positively to the message and turn to Christ in repentance and faith, only then am I able to say, 'Hey, welcome to the family, you're among the elect!' The American evangelist, D L Moody, put it like this, 'The whosoever-wills are the elect and the whosoever-won'ts are the non-elect.'

Glory to God

The impact of God's word upon people's lives and the ripening of the eternal purpose of God in our coming to faith and trust in him is brought out beautifully in *The Message*, 'It is clear to us, friends, that God not only loves you very much but also has put his hand on you for something special. When the message we preached came to you, it was not just words. Something happened in you. The Holy Spirit put steel in your convictions.'

- Salvation begins in the heart of God.
- Salvation encompasses the love of God.
- Salvation necessitates faith.
- Salvation involves the Trinity.
- Salvation transforms the life.

Those whom God chooses, God changes! They are not what they used to be, they are not yet what they are going to be, but thank God they are what they are by God's prodigious grace. The Welsh pastor, William Vernon Higham (1926-2016), sums it up better than I ever could:

Great is the gospel of our glorious God,
Where mercy met the anger of God's rod;
A penalty was paid and pardon bought,
And sinners lost at last to him were brought.

Similarly, the Methodist revivalist Charles Wesley (1707-88), revelled in this liberating experience:

Long my imprisoned spirit lay
Fast bound in sin and nature's night;
Thine eye diffused a quick'ning ray –
I woke, the dungeon flamed with light;
My chains fell off, my heart was free.
I rose, went forth, and followed thee.

That is what the biblical doctrine of election is all about. Every time I stop and think about it, I am bowled over with the thoroughgoing wonder of it all. I often cry out, 'O, the depth of the riches and wisdom and knowledge of God! How unsearchable are his judgments and how inscrutable his ways!' (Romans 11:33).

Spurgeon said on one unforgettable occasion in London's Metropolitan Tabernacle pulpit, 'If God hadn't chosen me before the creation of the world, he wouldn't choose me now!' When George MacDonald, the great Scottish preacher, told one of his children about the glories of God's grace, the child interrupted him and said, 'Dad, it all seems too good to be true.' A beaming smile spread across MacDonald's whiskered face as he answered back, 'Nay, my dear, it's just so good, it must be true!'

1:6

Excited about evangelism

The fervid zeal and enthusiasm of these relatively young Christians hits us between the eyes. We cannot help but be impressed by the unassailable fact that they are evangelistic. They passionately believed in outreach and were committed to sharing the gospel message with others near and far. Outreach is 'reaching out' because the church that does not reach out will pass out!

These gospel guys were overjoyed at the thought of their election, they were thrilled to bits with all that God did in their lives. They displayed a give all you can, hold nothing back attitude to evangelism. They had a heartthrob for people who did not know Jesus as Lord and Saviour.

They were chosen in Christ and this is what God used to give a razor-sharp cutting edge to their zealous endeavours to win men to Jesus. Theirs was a no-holds-barred, pull-out-all-the-stops, get-on-with-it mindset. Basically, they had a sense of responsibility to others, combined with a sense of accountability to God. The God who did so much for them, who captivated their affections, who was their everything and their all, yes, they were debtors to him, but they were out there on the front line paying their debt to all those still outside the family of God.

We are in the global family of God: we revel in that; we delight that we are found in such a happy, privileged position. They are not! We owe it to them to tell them of one who is 'mighty to save' (Isaiah 63:1). These folk were just as excited about election as they were about evangelism. As John Blanchard notes, 'In the Bible, election and evangelism meet with joined hands, not clenched fists.'

The copycat syndrome

The apostle pulls back the curtain another time and shows us more virtues of this thriving congregation of God's people. Paul talks about their experience. It can truly be said of them that they were men-followers, for we read, *you became imitators of us and of the Lord*. They began to follow the example as well as the teaching of the apostles. They walked in the footsteps of Paul and in so doing walked in harmony with Christ.

Paul and his ministry colleagues lived out the gospel before them. They came with very few answers, no verbal hot air, and a lot of vulnerability. They clothed the gospel with human skin, a kind of incarnational gospel at its best. They were glasshouse Christians, for people could see right through them; they had nothing to hide. No skeletons hanging in their closets, no hidden agendas. In computer-speak, what you see is what you get! They emulated Paul and his associates. They mimicked them and looked upon them as role models. Copycats. Paul must have had an unblemished testimony, a transparency to his character. He walked a straight line on the narrow path.

I do not know how you feel when you hear something like that. I know the impact it has on me, I find it immensely challenging. Our lives are real stories constantly read by people milling around us. We are walking sermons. I sometimes ask myself the question: When others follow me, where do I lead them? Am I a stepping stone, or a stumbling block? We are signposts on the highway of life, are we pointing men and women in the direction of Jesus? We are the Bible the world is reading. I wonder what translation they pick up when they read the book of my life?

Pointers to success

The secret lay in Paul's closeness to Christ. There was an intimacy to his dynamic relationship with the Lord; he was head over heels in love with Jesus. His communion is superb, for the channels of communication were wide open and there was no earth-born cloud between him and his God. His consecration is glowingly admirable. He was totally sold out to Jesus Christ, he surrendered everything to the lordship of Christ, and he had no quibbles or qualms about so doing. There are no hints of regret, no second thoughts. He holds nothing back because Jesus is number one on his personal agenda. Paul's priorities were sorted out on bended knees before the cross.

It is apparent when they looked at Paul, they saw Jesus. Paul was a leader and they gladly followed. Surely the avowed aim of any Christian leader is to win souls, but equally important, according to Hebrews 13:17, is to 'watch' over their souls. That is the role of a pastor or elder in every gospel church.

Stand up, stand up for Jesus

It was not a cushy number being a Christian in their day. Nevertheless, they nailed their colours to the mast. They willingly counted the cost and gladly paid the price. Even though it cost them nothing to become a Christian, it would cost them everything to be one. There was nothing comfortable about their Christianity. They were not laid-back in any way.

There were whopping great pressures. The psychological stress was at times unbearable. The constant emotional strain meant they were on the verge of cracking up. Their nerves were frayed. They felt zapped. The going was tough, an endurance test, a real struggle from dawn to dusk. It was not all plain sailing. Actually, truth be told, their backs were to the wall as they stood at wit's-end corner. When lesser men would have given up and given in, and feebler men would have tossed the towel into the ring and called it quits, they *received the word in much affliction.*

They received the word with gladness because they really loved the word of God. They rejoiced in its proclamation. Quite frankly, they could not get enough of it. A dream congregation for every preacher! They were hungry for gospel truth, drinking in every word that was spoken, and sitting on the edge of their seats. And they kept coming back for more.

How were they able to do it? Well, says Paul, *with the joy of the Holy Spirit.* Their circumstances were not conducive to such a positive response. Humanly speaking, the odds were stacked against them. The dominoes were falling. But they had joy – real joy, wonderful joy – a joy deep down in their hearts. Happiness depends on what happens to us, but come what may, there is jubilation in knowing Jesus. An inward glee, an exuberance of spirit, an overflowing heart; it is the cup of our life full and running over. 'Joy is the standard that flies on the battlements of the heart when the King is in residence,' comments Leonard Small.

Sure, the trials were there, they did not go away. The intense heat was felt, and it was going to get hotter. But, as only the Lord can, he makes it up to them in another way. Their lives are richer. They are buoyant and bullish, even though all is sinking around them. God never shortchanges his people. They discovered that 'the joy of the Lord [was their] strength' (Nehemiah 8:10). Their experience contained the transforming power of the Holy Spirit and the living vitality of the risen Christ. That explains why they were able to hold out for as long as they did and hold on in the manner they did!

1:7

An ecclesiastical prototype

Experience is one thing, example is another. They became a model church. A gospel church. Paul expressed it superbly when he wrote, *so that you became an example to all the believers in Macedonia and in Achaia.* This is quite something! No other church in the New Testament is referred to in this way, so let us give credit where it is due. It is an honour to be hailed as a pattern worth adopting. They got it right. First time. They were not perfect, but they were ideal. They made their mark and left a lasting impression. They were an excellent advertisement of biblical Christianity. Theirs is an example to be embraced with open hands and open hearts. They were not in a rut, but they had a mould.

When we read between the lines it appears that throughout the region and further afield people were sitting up and taking notice. J Ligon Duncan says, 'It is the church that makes the gospel visible.' They were looking over their shoulders and saying, 'Hey, do you see what they are doing up there in Thessalonica, why don't we adapt it, why don't we customise it, let's have a go ourselves.' Or perhaps they may have said, 'If it works over there, we've nothing to lose, let's give it a try and see if it'll work down here.' It is the 'nothing ventured, nothing gained' syndrome. They made all the running and others jumped aboard the gravy train. They were pacesetters for their day and generation, people who had the vision to push the limits of faith because they themselves lived on the raw edge of faith. This would indicate that in a constantly changing situation there was a willingness to adapt. There was a degree of flexibility in the fellowship as they geared to the times, but remained anchored to the word.

The ripple effect

From up north in the province of Macedonia and down south to the province of Achaia, there was a real sense that God was doing some new thing among them. Believe it or not, these believers were a catalyst in the wider community of gospel people. All of Greece was influenced to a greater or lesser degree by the church that gathered in the vicinity of Thessalonica as there was something exceptionally special about them. They were a beacon of light, for theirs was a radiant testimony and a shining witness as they impacted their peers. Shimmering saints. Luminous believers.

The thinking that governed their missional strategy is summed up in two familiar words, 'shake' and 'shine'. The same philosophy is expressed in Matthew 5:13-16 in *The Message* where Jesus challenges us to bring out the 'God-flavours' of this earth and the 'God-colours' in this world. That is what gospel people do best!

1:8

Sharing your faith

What did they do? They had a message to share, a story to tell. Let me tell you what they did not do – they did not do what most of us probably would have done and form a committee to organise a special big-money, star-studded event with some celebrity preacher. Instead, they rallied the troops and got on with it themselves! We read, *the word of the Lord sounded forth from you.* They were partisan to evangelism. The *you* is personal – it is as individual as it can be, and at the same time, it is corporate, for none are left out. There is no exclusion clause. There was no way any of them could opt out if they did not feel like it or feel up to it.

They were reaching their friends, neighbours, and colleagues with the greatest story ever told. The old adage remains relevant to this day: across the street, around the world. Their faith was believable and they knew how to give it away. They all had something to say. O yes, they could blether about the weather, the rate of inflation, and the escalating price of all kinds of consumer goods, they could rattle on about everything under the sun, but they also had plenty to say when it came to talking about the Lord Jesus. Every member of the body of Christ was functioning efficiently and effectively. To a man they were mobilised in the army of the Lord. They just wanted to lobby for God.

Churches grow when Christians evangelise. Sometimes we act as if we do not really believe that! It is estimated that 75-80% of new converts are brought to faith in Christ by the favourable influence of someone they already know. It is about building bridges to walk over, rather than constructing high-rise barricades. It is about making friends with people so that we can introduce them to the best friend of all, and making sure that our actions match our words for what we do speaks louder than what we say.

Take a moment, think outside the box with regard to the possibilities and potential in your church if something similar were to take place. The won't-go-away fact is, God loved Thessalonica and so did they!

Transmitting the truth

- It involves a measure of preparation – we have to learn how best to do it and we cannot beat on-the-job training.

- It involves a degree of partnership – we are in it together, it is not individuals blowing their own trumpet.

- It involves a hint of progress – the idea is to go forward and not stand still or mark time.

- It involves a note of purity – when the trumpet sounds, clarity is of the essence.

We may choose to make the presentation more upmarket by bringing the style that we adopt into the twenty-first century. There is wisdom in going down that road. It makes a lot of sense, for we must be relevant! Paul said elsewhere that it is 'by all means' that we save some (1 Corinthians 9:22). Having said that, the gospel message is just the same today as it was back then. The story of Calvary is timeless, changeless, and eternal.

No uncertain sound

The thought inherent in the phrase *sounded forth* is the noise which comes from a resounding gong or a roaring sea. It can also be likened to the sound of a loud trumpet or the noise generated from a great clap of thunder. This is the only time this word appears in the Greek New Testament. The implication is, at all events, whether Paul is thinking of thunder or trumpets, the gospel proclaimed by the believers in Thessalonica made such a loud noise that it reverberated throughout the hills and valleys of Greece.

Actually, they did such a splendid job that no matter where Paul went he was sure to hear, 'Some Thessalonians already gave us that message, they have told us about your Jesus.' Today, we are a media-conscious, media-savvy generation, we know the power of the mass media on the public mindset – talk to any advertising agency – so we seek to use it to its fullest potential. Nothing wrong with that!

By the same token, there is another way and it is a route implicit in Paul's wise comments in this verse. The chances are this way is even more effective than blanket coverage of the message on a global scale. This way requires no complicated electronic gadgetry, it is unbelievably simple. It is neither organised nor computerised, it is spontaneous. It is not hugely expensive, in fact, it costs precisely nothing. We might call it, holy conversation.

God's gossipers

A gospel conversation is the transmission from one person to another person, of the impact that the good news of Jesus is making on people. It happens when Mrs Jones meets Mr Brown and they strike up an animated chit-chat at the bus stop or supermarket checkout, or when Sally and Dave get together for a confab and cappuccino. It sounds like this: 'Have you heard what's happened to so-and-so? They're not the same! Did you know that such-and-such a person has gone all religious and believed in God? I tell you, something extraordinary is going on in Thessalonica, it's all change! People are different. Their attitude is different. They're into faith, love, and hope in a big way.'

The result of such gratuitous publicity is enough to blow the cobwebs from your mind. Comprehensive. Beyond our wildest dreams. As John Bertram Phillips (1906-82) translates in his *New Testament in Modern English*, 'We do not need to tell other people about it, other people tell us.' Not only was the media redundant, the missionaries felt redundant too! The bottom line is this: the message was spreading like wildfire without them!

Up-and-at-'em

It was all hands on deck evangelism! How quickly the gospel would spread if each of us would do what these folk did two millennia ago. When it comes to witnessing, sometimes we are like goldfish: we open and close our mouths and nothing comes out! They could not keep it to themselves because they caught a vision of a world without Jesus. A vision that captured their imagination then conquered their hearts. Like my missionary friends in SIM, they were 'convinced that no one should live or die without hearing God's good news!'

Like a mighty oak, the gospel church at Thessalonica stood strong against the harsh winds of chilling persecution and ice-cold apathy, she spread her branches of faith throughout the world. They were top-class heralds telling others they knew Jesus saves, because he did it for them and no one could refute or deny their testimony. 'I was there when it happened, so I ought to know' was the mindset. They were highly effective in their outreach because they themselves were infected and impacted. Their mandate is summed up in four words: each one, reach one.

What about the message they passed on? It was:

- a pure gospel – Christ and nothing else
- a full gospel – Christ and nothing less
- a plain gospel – Christ and nothing more

This was sensationally good news in a mad, bad, sad world. It is the gospel as it really is. It sounded out, but first they started where they were, at home in their own backyard, and only then did they venture further afield. Sounds like the Acts 1:8 principle put into practice, the ripple-in-the-pond syndrome.

Talk of the town

Their ministry of propagation transcended their own city, and region, and nation. Its tentacles reached out far beyond their geographical boundaries to ultimately have an international scope. It has been well said that 'in just about one year, a new church with first generation believers was experiencing a ministry whose proportions matched those of Christ's great commission.' God intends every local church to be like the church in Thessalonica; as John Stott says, the risen Lord wants us 'to be like a sounding board, bouncing off the vibrations of the gospel, or like a telecommunications satellite which first receives and then transmits the message.'

Across the land, people were passing comments about the wee gospel church at Thessalonica, chatting about their faith in God. That was the focal point of many an enlightened conversation. Jesus was front-page news!

Why? Because they were fired-up. They heard the word of God and they could not wait until they passed it on to others. They were not sitting up in the bleachers, they were down on the field of play. Not for them the indulgence of sitting on a park bench or a sandy beach, they were in the starting line-up. Their hearts were burning with the life-changing message of Jesus Christ. Saints with loads of vim and a good dose of sanctified panache!

Such persecution as they endured could so easily have smothered the gospel flame. Instead, it was like pouring petrol on a burning match. Their suffering fuelled a fire that exploded into an even greater commitment to evangelism. They were evangelical and evangelistic. Their united testimony was an expression of vibrant, authentic Christianity in action. I read recently that 'faith is like calories. We cannot see them, but we can always see the results!'

The onus is on us

If we were willing to adopt a similar attitude to theirs, before long our church would be renowned as a hotbed of evangelism. We would be the talk of the town for all the right reasons, when we reach out and sound out, and with the Lord on our side, get up and go out. Never forget that

God has placed us where he has placed no one else! As Elsie Yale's (1873-1956) song says, 'There's a work for Jesus, none but you can do!'

As long as one person does not know Jesus, our work is not finished. We do not have the luxury of folding our arms and resting on the laurels of past success. It is a case of every church, every member, every hand reaching the unreached and least-reached. There is no other way to reach the world for Jesus. God's heart beats with a passion to save lost sinners.

From that dreadfully dark day when sin separated him from his creation, a gracious God has been faithfully reaching out to mankind. Persistently. Like a distraught father searching for a wayward son or daughter, he has been calling out to the world ever since. He does not speak through a temple in Jerusalem or a nation *in situ* today; he speaks through a redeemed people. We are the megaphone through which he lovingly pleads with the world to be saved, because the gospel is not just for domestic consumption, it is also for export. In light of all we have seen of the early church, let us remember, the same God who fanned the flame in the first century can ignite a blaze in our hearts in the twenty-first century. Are we willing to let him?

1:9

Bondslave

Paul pulls no punches when he writes, *For they themselves report concerning us the kind of reception we had among you, and how you turned to God from idols to serve the living and true God.* In one sense this is a paradox for they were set free in order to find perfect liberty in serving Jesus. Their goal in life is God. Born of God, blessed by God, now they show how enriching it is to be bound to God. The hymn writer expressed it well:

> *My goal is God himself,*
> *Not joy, nor peace,*
> *Nor even blessing,*
> *But himself, my God:*
> *'Tis his to lead me there,*
> *Not mine, but his,*
> *'At any cost, dear Lord, by any road.'*

For them, the price was high – the suffering: intense and severe; the cost: king-sized; the pressure was really piling on, thick and fast. The bumpy road down which they meandered was renowned for its twists and turns and a plethora of obstacles strewn across it. Yet their number one goal in life is unchanged: God. Why is that their upbeat attitude to life? When bad things are happening to good people, why are they still on track? Why have they not lost their keenness to serve Jesus? The answer is found in a delightful story told by Jesus where the punchline is, 'the man who is forgiven much is the man who loves much' (Luke 7:36-50). The more we stop and think about it and the more we look at the gospel church in Thessalonica, the more we realise this was certainly true of them.

Emancipation

Conversion is not worth the paper it is written on if it is not a life-changing experience. An internal revolution. It is something so radical that it causes men to march to the beat of a different drum. An about-turn, a change of direction. Such transformation drives home the truth that God's grace is too amazing to save us from sin's guilt only to leave us under its cruel tyranny. John Walvoord underlines this gospel phenomenon with this observation, 'When we put our trust in Jesus Christ, we transfer from the road to Armageddon to the road to Glory.'

It is a personal encounter with the living God, and when man meets God one-to-one, he is never the same again. Their conversion bears dramatic testimony to the miraculous touch of God upon their lives. Enough to take the breath away. Conversion is an experience which happens in a moment that lasts for a lifetime.

We read that they *turned to God*. That is what theologians refer to as repentance. We go on to read in the next phrase that they *turned to God from idols*. That is separation. Initially, they made a choice followed by a change of heart, mind, and will. It was a change of life coupled with a change of lifestyle. Not a refurbishment project or a spiritual makeover. You see, when a person comes to *know* Jesus, they will *know* change and if there is *no* change, there is likely *no* Jesus (2 Corinthians 13:5).

There was a plus factor in that they turned their hearts toward the Lord. The minus factor in the equation was when they turned their backs on idols. By and large they were converts from paganism. The idols in question were images of a tangible kind, man-made statues intended to represent the deities supposed to reside on Mount Olympus. When these heathens turned in childlike faith to the Lord, they repudiated their former allegiance to such fatuous vanities.

Burning bridges

They did not turn to God because they were disillusioned with life, nor because they felt they had suffered enough, nor because they were fed up with all that life was throwing their way, nor because they were at the end of their tether and living their lives on the flip side. Certainly not! In Mark Howell's words, 'The Thessalonians did not merely *try on* Jesus to see if he would fit into the wardrobe of their lives. Instead, they *clothed themselves* completely with him (Romans 13:14).'

It was the unimpeachable character of the one true God that won them over. And it is always that way. Before his gloriousness everything else pales into insignificance and nothingness, for he is unrivalled. Peerless. In his 24-carat light all else fades into oblivion. Salvation does not begin when we give up something, it begins when we receive someone. And that is precisely what they did!

- They turned to the *living* God for he is not dead, he is alive!
- They turned to the *true* God for he is not deceitful, he is real!

The psalmist reminds us in Psalm 115:5-7 that idols have eyes but they cannot see, ears but they cannot hear, feet but they cannot walk, hands but they cannot touch, and bodies but they cannot feel.

It would be difficult to exaggerate the impact the gospel had on them. The contrast is unreal: idols are dead, God is living; idols are false, God is true; idols are many, God is one; idols are visible and tangible, God is invisible and intangible, beyond the reach of sight and touch. In the wider sense, an icon – a sacred cow – could easily be defined as a God substitute. An injection of God-replacement therapy.

The number of things that a sophisticated person may put in God's place is legion. Whatever we spend most of our time thinking about becomes our god! Some of us make an idol of a career, others make an idol of their home. The fast car, the latest technology, the jet-set lifestyle, or for that matter, any other designer label or must-have accessory – all these can easily be promoted in our minds to the status of deity, a god we lovingly and adoringly worship. In that sense every convert to the faith of Jesus turns away from idols.

Aiden Wilson Tozer (1897-1963) said that 'the essence of idolatry is thinking thoughts of God that are unworthy of him.' If we are honest, the overwhelming majority of us have been guilty of making idols which dominate our devotion, govern our duties, influence our decisions, dictate the things we like and dislike, when all of the time, in our life, ministry, and church, it should be God plus nothing! Charles Stanley, President of In Touch Ministries, hits the nail on the head when he writes, 'An idol is anything you value more – either by your attitude or actions – than God.'

That was a lesson they learned well in Thessalonica. This may be an opportune moment for us to pray along with William Cowper:

The dearest idol I have known,
Whate'er that idol be,
Help me to tear it from thy throne,
And worship only thee.

Things are different now

Look what happened to them! See the stupendous difference. They were dead in sin; now they are alive in God. They were living in pitch black darkness; now they are walking in translucent light. A brand-new creation. A spiritual metamorphosis. For them, and for us, it is new life in Christ. As Steven Lawson of One Passion Ministries says, 'The greatest life anyone can live is to live for Jesus Christ. Any other life is not even living but merely existing.'

How true it is that no testimony is quite so compelling as that of a changed life. People can argue theology and dispute translations of the Bible until they are blue in the face, but they are rendered speechless when confronted with the reality of a transformed life. It is 'the unarguable apologetic'. Brennan Manning is spot on when he admitted that 'it's hard to be a Christian, but it's too dull to be anything else.' Their testimony is summed up in the words of Rufus Henry McDaniel's (1850-1940) song:

What a wonderful change in my life has been wrought
Since Jesus came into my heart!
I have light in my soul for which long I had sought,
Since Jesus came into my heart!

The emphasis here is on a God who is *living and true*, and when we compare this with a host of other comments dotted throughout the New Testament, we can say that Christians are children of the living God, their body becomes the temple of the living God, they are indwelt by the Spirit of the living God, they become an integral part of the church of the living God, and for it he is preparing even now the city of the living God. Wow!

We joyfully sing with Rob Hayward, 'I'm accepted, I'm forgiven, I am fathered by the true and living God.' Or again, we gladly affirm with Dave Bilbrough, 'I am a new creation, no more in condemnation, here in the grace of God I stand.'

Saved to serve

Saved, they definitely were. But why? Well, their motto is summed up in the well-worn cliché: saved to serve! That was their primary occupation, their *labour of love* (1:3). They were captivated by Christ. Enraptured with Jesus.

The word *serve* introduces the picture of a bondslave, one so devoted and dedicated to his master that he wants to be his servant all his days (Deuteronomy 15:12-17). He loves the Lord as his Master. It is in slavery to Christ that he finds true liberty and freedom. A paradox, but gloriously true.

Scotsman George Matheson (1842-1906) echoes a similar sentiment when he writes, 'Make me a captive, Lord, and then I shall be free.' The bondslave declares by his actions, I have no rights, it is all down to the plan of my master; and I have no will, except it is one with his.

That goes against the modern trend. It is not in vogue. It takes an awful lot of assiduousness to go down that road. Too often we are like the young man who poured out his heart's devotion in a love letter to the girl of his dreams. He wrote, 'Darling, I love you so much that I would climb the highest mountain, swim the widest stream, cross the burning desert, die at the stake for you. By the way, I'll see you on Saturday if it doesn't rain.'

Commitment! Regrettably, one word rarely found in Christianese in the third millennium. Ask any pastor. It embraces a firm dedication to each other in the family of God, a lifelong devotion to the Lord Jesus and his great service, and a total loyalty and diligence to the local church and her various ministries. Commitment says 'no' to me and 'yes' to Jesus!

1:10

A growing sense of expectancy

Here is the climax of our personal faith in the living and true God. This is, unquestionably, hope with a capital HOPE. It is the moment for which we were chosen, the ultimate experience for all the redeemed of the Lord. Future grace. Future glory.

The question needs to be asked: What are they doing? We glean from verses 9 and 10 that serving and waiting go hand in hand in the experience of gospel people. At first sight this is a little surprising since serving is active while waiting is passive. In Christian terms, serving is getting busy for Jesus on earth, while waiting is looking for our Lord to come from heaven. And, yet, these two are not strange bedfellows. They are buddies!

Each beautifully balances the other. On one hand, however hard we work and serve, there are limits to what we accomplish and achieve. We can only improve society, we cannot perfect it. We shall never build Utopia on this earth. For that, we have to wait for Christ to come. Only then will he secure the final triumph of God's reign of justice and peace.

On the other hand, although we must look expectantly for the advent of Jesus, we have no liberty to wait in idleness, with arms folded and eyes closed, indifferent to the needs of the world around us. Instead, we must work even while we wait, for we are called *to serve the living and true God*.

Worth waiting for

It is most interesting to note that Paul says, they are *to wait for his Son from heaven*. The Greek word translated *wait* is used only here in the entire New Testament where it has the thought of anticipation or expectation associated with it. A similar idea is found in Paul's insightful comments in Philippians 3:20 and Titus 2:13. It rings with the idea of the prophetic hope that things on earth will not always continue the way they are currently; that is another angle on the phrase *steadfastness of hope* which Paul used at the top of the chapter in verse 3.

This is what makes the Christian life really worth living, for we have something to live for today and so much to look forward to in all our tomorrows. We have a distinct edge over the average man on the street. When tomorrow comes, and it will, we expect a bright one. We know the best is yet to be. We are convinced that one day, sooner rather than later, we shall see the Lord in his flawless beauty. One glorious morning the clouds will be swept aside, the shadows will have flown, and we shall rise to be with Jesus. An exhilarating, mouth-watering prospect! No wonder the hymn writer William Cowper (1731-1800) wrote:

> *How thou can'st think so well of me,*
> *And be the God thou art;*
> *Is darkness to my intellect,*
> *But sunshine to my heart.*

We live every day knowing that Jesus could be back before another day dawns. Today, we see a poor reflection as in a mirror; then, face to face. Paul writes in 1 Corinthians 13:12 in *The Message*, 'We don't yet see things clearly. We're squinting in a fog, peering through a mist. But it won't be long before the weather clears and the sun shines brightly! We'll see it all then, see it all as clearly as God sees us, knowing him directly just as he knows us!'

Looking out, looking up

These first-century gospel people were not hanging around on every street corner idling the hours away, or sitting back on a leather chair twiddling their thumbs, or relaxing on a deckchair waiting for it all to happen. 'They were not just part of a religion locked out of time and space, drifting aimlessly across the landscape of humanity,' writes David Jeremiah.

Their future orientation to life is what energised their present service. They were zealously working flat out for the Lord. Like John Wesley they wanted to be 'up and doing for Jesus'. They really believed in their hearts that the Lord's return could happen at any moment. Impending. Imminent. Yes, for them, it was as close as that. For us, two thousand years further down the road, how much nearer it is. The reality is, like the village clock that kept on chiming, it has never been so late before!

They looked forward with a real sense of expectancy to the advent of Jesus. They were watching for the appearing of the Lord from heaven, passionately longing for him to break through the clouds. They avidly read the signs of the times and the cry went up from fast-beating hearts, 'How long, O Lord, how long?'

The fact is, Jesus is coming. Coming soon! Coming suddenly! We do not know when, but we know it will happen. Guaranteed. John Ross Macduff (1818-95) voiced those sentiments when he wrote:

With that blessed hope before us,
Let our joyful songs be sung;
Let the mighty advent chorus
Onward roll from tongue to tongue.
Christ is coming!
Come, Lord Jesus, quickly come!

Up, up, and away

When Christ returns he will *deliver us from the wrath to come*. His is a rescue mission that will not be botched. No matter which way we look at it, it will be eminently successful. Deliverance is the order of the day. The *wrath to come* could refer to a couple of significant events. Number one, it could speak of the frightening eternal judgment of God. Number two, it could refer initially to the period of seven years tribulation upon Planet Earth. This is what Joel called 'the great and terrible day of the Lord' (Joel 2:31). The prophet Jeremiah described it as the 'day of Jacob's trouble' (Jeremiah 30:7). Jesus spoke of it in his highly-acclaimed Olivet discourse as 'the great tribulation' (Matthew 24:21; *cf.* Revelation 6-16). It is cosmic. Global. All hell is let loose with the devil and his angels on the rampage in a reign of terror. It is one calamity hard on the heels of another, a classic case of going from bad to worse. A vortex of evil. A downward spiral of sin.

Yes, the Lord will come and snatch us away. The one who plucked us as brands from the burning will at the end of the day return for us to take us safely home to glory. That implies that the true church of God will not enter or go through the period of tribulation. I believe this is alluded to elsewhere in 1 Thessalonians where Paul says in 5:9 that *God has not destined us for wrath, but to obtain salvation through our Lord Jesus Christ.*

All's well that ends well

These early believers were working, watching, and waiting. The word used by Paul is in the present tense which means they were living today in light of tomorrow. Eternity was etched on their hearts and the thought of it occupied every waking moment. They lived for it and were prepared to die for it.

They were numbered among those who 'love his appearing' (2 Timothy 4:8). They were standing on the tiptoe of expectancy, waiting up for him, for he could be back at any moment. They were watching out for him, peeking behind the curtains. Like them, our future is as bright as the promises of God.

What a delightful group, a gospel fellowship where people believed in the second coming of the Lord Jesus. Believe it or not, they were excited about eschatology (doctrine of last things), for all the right reasons. Samuel Trevor Francis (1834-1925) captured the mood and mystique of that moment when he wrote:

I am waiting for the coming
Of the Lord who died for me;
O his words have thrilled my spirit,
'I will come again for thee.'

I can almost hear his footfall
On the threshold of the door,
And my heart, my heart is longing
To be with him evermore.

Perhaps today

On one of my American ministry trips I was privileged to preach in the great city of Grand Rapids, Michigan. Aside from meeting some wonderful people along the way, a highlight for me was a visit to the global headquarters of Our Daily Bread Ministries (formerly known as Radio Bible Class) founded in 1938 by Dr Martin Ralph DeHaan (1891-1965). He also co-edited the well-loved monthly devotional booklet, *Our Daily Bread.*

Next stop on my schedule was the nearby Woodlawn Cemetery, as I was keen to visit DeHaan's grave. Underneath an appropriate text from Scripture, a simple, capitalised message adorns his granite headstone – PERHAPS TODAY.

The challenge for us is unmistakably clear: yes, we are ready for heaven, but are we ready to meet the Lord? I invite you to join me in saying, 'Perhaps today!'

A church where discipleship is modelled

The young pastor had just announced to his congregation that he was leaving. He was standing at the door after the service, greeting his congregation, when one of the elderly saints approached him, her eyes swimming with tears. She sobbed and said, 'Pastor, I'm so sorry you've decided to leave. Things will never be the same again.' The young man was flattered but was equal to the situation. He clasped her hands in his and replied most graciously, 'Bless you, my dear, but I'm sure the Lord will send you a new pastor even better than I.' Choking with emotion, she said, 'That's what they all say, but they keep getting worse and worse.'

Postnatal care

Any parent will tell you that it is one thing having a baby; it is quite a different matter seeing that kid grow up! That is what this chapter is all about: a gospel church being nurtured in the faith. We saw Paul in the role of evangelist in chapter one, now we meet him in a pastoral capacity.

The abiding value of this chapter (and the next) is the remarkable insight it gives into Paul's heart, as it is a crystalline window on what makes him tick. In these chapters, more perhaps than anywhere else in his letters, Paul discloses his mind, what he thinks, his prime reason for getting out of bed in the morning; he expresses his emotions, the joys and sorrows of ministry, for he wears his heart on his sleeve; and he bares his soul as he shares some of his most intimate dreams and fears.

Paul saw himself as an undershepherd of the flock of God, someone to look after the lambs and share Christ with the sheep and to ultimately bring everyone into a deeper understanding of the means of grace. Every pastor to God's flock is given the command, 'do the work of an evangelist' (2 Timothy 4:5). From reading between the lines, it is clear that Paul was not only good on theory, for he also practised what he preached. There is a weight of clear-cut evidence amassed in his favour that it was through his biblical preaching that the church in Thessalonica was founded. To his credit, and for God's glory, it was through his faithful shepherding that this infant gospel church progressed as well as she did, and as far as she did, down the road to spiritual maturity.

That is the difference between commitment to Christ and consecration to Christ. The Keswick Convention preacher, Alan Redpath (1907-89), noted that 'the conversion of a soul is the miracle of a moment, the manufacture of a saint is the task of a lifetime.' It is one thing to start a race, the challenge is to keep on track and then with arms aloft cross the finish line. Sadly, the long and chequered history of the church confirms that many fall out on the last lap.

As we begin to carefully unpack the teaching in this chapter, we discover some unbelievable insights into the lifestyle of the apostle and his philosophy of ministry. This true servant of God was characterised by integrity, devotion, and total allegiance to Christ, all harnessed to a life of discipline. The missionary statesman, James Hudson Taylor (1832-1905), has written that 'a person may be dedicated and devoted, but if he is ill-disciplined, he will be useless.'

2:1

A ministry-driven church

The apostle, with both hands, seizes the opportunity to remind them of the kind of gospel ministry he exercised among them. Here we see how Paul approached ministry. He paints five pictures, thumbnail sketches, of his overall ministry, on the canvas of Scripture:

- his rejoicing as a reaper (verse 1)
- his purpose as a preacher (verses 2-6)
- his nature as a nurse (verses 7-8)
- his saintliness as a servant (verses 9-10)
- his faithfulness as a father (verses 11-12)

In so doing, Paul has given us a vignette of the role he occupied when he was with them. He exercised, in the familiar words of an outstanding Baptist preacher of a bygone era, C H Spurgeon, 'an all-round ministry'.

Handling his critics

Paul is stepping up to the plate and the reason why is not too hard to see. No defensive batting for Paul, he is swinging for the fences! Some of these fifth-columnists were pointing an accusing finger at him, others were spreading scandalous stories about him, a few were trying to undermine his entire ministry – whatever way we look at it, some were so determined to discredit him that they launched a malicious smear campaign against him.

'The preacher man ran away,' they sneered, 'and wonder of wonders, he hasn't been seen or heard of since. He's just another one of a long line of phoney teachers who tramp up and down the Egnatian Way. This guy's in the job only for what he can get out of it in terms of sex, money, prestige, and power. So when red-hot opposition arose and he found himself boxed in, he took to his heels and ran, you couldn't see him for dust. He doesn't give two cents for you; he's left you to fend for yourselves. Don't be so naïve, he's much more concerned about his own skin than your welfare!'

There is no way Paul was going to take that scurrilous nonsense on the chin. They were not going to treat him like a doormat. Hating people is like burning down your own house to get rid of a rat. As soon as he became aware of the raucous rumblings, he went into firefighting mode and moved quickly to extinguish the flames. He wants to do all he can, as fast as he can, to quell the ridiculous rumours and bolster the church.

Some of the more gullible, easily-led folk were probably carried away by this torrent of abuse. The twin facts of Paul's abrupt departure and his failure to return seemed to fit the accusations being levelled against him. On the surface their case sounded pretty plausible, even convincing.

Paul must have found this personal attack extremely painful and unnerving. In all fairness, he does not allow it to colour his thinking, nor does he permit it to cloud his perception. He knows he has to respond to the charges, and when he does, it is not out of pique or vanity, it is because the truth of the gospel and the future of the church are at stake. He voluntarily goes on the record and says, 'Let the facts speak for themselves.'

- their impeccable character (verses 1-7)
- their unimpeachable conduct (verses 8-12)

Cooking the books?

What a thrilling story. Front-page news. Inches of editorial column. This is really sensational. This first-century Billy Graham spent three weeks, give or take a day or two, with them, and as a result of his noteworthy efforts, a gospel church was started. Paul oozes confidence for he knows his track record speaks for itself. He does not juggle the statistics to make them look better than they really are; he does not have to, he does not need to.

Sometimes there is a great gap between what we think others think about us and what others *really* think about us. Paul says quite categorically that, in spite of what other people might say, including the cynics and critics sniping from the relative safety of the sidelines, they all know in their heart of hearts that his visit to them was a runaway, rip-roaring success. It was a resoundingly positive experience; by no stretch of the imagination was it a failure.

A God-blessed ministry

No sooner has Paul cleared his chest than he turns on his accusers by asking them a penetrating question. Pointing to those who have been born again under his anointed ministry, he asks: What's that? There is only one possible answer, it is God giving the increase. Paul's labours were well and truly rewarded. Famously so. He looked back with no tinge of sadness and no hint of regret. He was buoyant because the Lord performed a series of miracles in northern Greece. His visit had not been unfruitful or unproductive. It had a measurable goal, and with God's deluge of blessing, that was achieved and accomplished. Our obligation is to always do the right thing, the rest is in God's hands.

In moments like these, it is opportune to recall the sentiments of the saintly Samuel Rutherford (1600-61) expressed in letter form, as a prisoner in the granite city of Aberdeen, and later distilled into poetic verse by Anne Ross Cousin (1824-1906). These were reflections on his pastoral charge in rural Galloway in southwest Scotland:

Fair Anwoth by the Solway, to me thou still art dear,
E'en on the verge of heaven, I drop for thee a tear,
O, if one soul from Anwoth, meet me at God's right hand,
My heaven will be two heavens, in Immanuel's land.

2:2

Not all sunshine

Paul gives us a breathtaking glimpse into what life was like for a travelling evangelist in his day. Any preacher worth his salt with an expanding and fruitful itinerant ministry was often hunted and hounded. Frequently beaten up and left lying in a ditch at the side of the road, they were just another statistic on the missing persons list. More often than not they were hauled before the courts to face trumped-up charges. Regularly they were thrown out of city and town with the label 'undesirable' attached.

If we were to trace Paul's journeys it would be like tracking the path of a wounded deer running from a hunter, leaving one bloody trail after another. Sometimes we are inclined to forget that this was Europe two thousand years ago. Paul talks openly and honestly about his persecution. He does not embellish it in any way, he does not exaggerate; he tells it for what it is. With clinical precision, he explains and exposes what happened at Philippi.

He and Silas were stripped and savagely beaten, then unceremoniously thrown into prison with their feet fastened in the stocks. It was an extremely painful and humiliating experience. In spite of their Roman citizenship, they were flogged naked in public, without trial. Both men were physically abused and suffered badly at the hands of others. They were grossly insulted, endured deprivation, and underwent systematic mental torture. They went through the proverbial mill.

In spite of all the harassment and belittlement he encountered, he pressed on. He battled on. Soldiered on. He resolutely moved ahead, nothing daunted or deterred him. He was willing to go the distance for and with the people he served. It winded him for he had been treated like a punchbag, but when he recovered his breath, he was back on the road! Battered, bruised, and bleeding, it would take a lot more than that to put him off. Nothing yellow-bellied about him. It proves that Paul was no self-serving religious fraud, or rogue preacher, or charlatan with ten suits, ten shirts, ten ties, and ten sermons.

Déjà vu

In the gracious providence of God that is how the missionaries happened to find themselves in Thessalonica, where it was a case of more of the same! Paul did not simply arrive in town because it was a port in a storm or because it was a convenient place to hole up and lick his wounds. It could never be said of him that he was a piece of human flotsam washed up in Macedonia by a tidal wave of events.

There was an explicit purpose behind it all. This guy believed in the sovereignty of God as one who overrules. He came as a man with a mission, and for him, as well as the locals, this was a defining moment. In Acts 16:40 he brought a measure of comfort to the saints at Philippi and encouraged them; in Acts 17:1-10 he brought the gospel of Christ to the sinners in Thessalonica and evangelised them.

How was he able to keep going? What was his secret? The answer is seen in a fresh, new light in the middle of verse 2 where the main beam is on divine power, 'the help of our God' (NIV). He was not trusting or relying on past success or academic ability, nor was he depending on the arm of flesh. His strength lay in the Lord enabling him to be what he wanted him to be. God undertook for him. And so with bravery and boldness he preached Jesus. The wonderful thing about it is that God never let him down. Not twice, not even once! When all is said and done, how could he? He is God!

Dare to be a ...

There is a mighty phrase employed in this verse that reinforces the kind of man that Paul really was. It says, *we had boldness in our God to declare to you.* He dared for the Lord Jesus. He was bold in jail and out of jail. He took his boldness in God into every arena of his life, such is the calibre of this man. He was no Johnny-come-lately. He was no theorising professor in a ten-feet-above-contradiction ivory tower. He was in the thick of it, down where the action was.

The odds were stacked high against him since he was deep in enemy territory, in the trenches, operating in a stronghold of Satan. Still he dared. He faced the opposition head-on in an eyeball-to-eyeball confrontation. Paul and his team pulled no punches as they squared up to them. They took their hands out of their pockets, rolled up their sleeves, and knocked the enemy out cold. No messing around here, there is a job to be done! Alistair Cooke reminds us that 'the great need for anyone in authority is courage.'

Feisty? Yes. Courageous? Yes. Spunky? Yes. Pertinacious? Yes. Men, ordinary men? Yes. They were men with big hearts for the Lord and a burning passion aflame in their breasts. Not unlike Joshua, Jeremiah, and the lesser-known Micaiah (Joshua 1:6-9; Jeremiah 1:8-19; 1 Kings 22:1-14). Their philosophy is summed up in the familiar adage of 'no pain, no gain, no cross, no crown'.

2:3

Too many Indians, not enough chiefs

There is a great premium on godly leadership these days. Most people in the average congregation realise that there are fewer leaders than are needed and fewer faithful leaders than are expected. We also know that leadership is colossally difficult. Many of us have been there and done that! In football, for example, when the team fails to win because they cannot put the ball in the back of the opposition's net, the board of directors sack the manager; in business, when employees do not deliver the goods, the shareholders call an extraordinary general meeting and fire the chief executive. Pronto!

The majority of us realise the need for capable, enthusiastic, inspiring leadership in the church. The bottom line is this: no matter where we look there is a leadership crisis prevalent in today's evangelical church. For one reason or another, the failure of many who are involved in gospel ministry seems to be a daily occurrence. It is not systemic, it just appears that way. The tragedy is there will be more high profile failures in the future!

The questions are: Knowing the subtlety of the enemy, how can spiritual leaders excel in competence? How can they have a genuine, lasting impact on other people's lives? How can they influence and shape their generation for the gospel, for God, and for good? How can they be history-makers?

The answer is found in these first half-dozen verses of chapter 2 where Paul shares some timeless principles for conducting an effective ministry! When it comes to doing church there is a handful of five ingredients that God signally honours and significantly blesses. Each of these relate to Paul's view of a wondrous God. He was:

- confident in God's power – giving him a gritty tenacity and a sense of being unbeatable

- committed to God's truth – giving him integrity and a sense of awesome responsibility

- commissioned by God's will – giving him authority and a sense of vocation

- compelled by God's knowledge – giving him accountability and a sense of security

- consumed with God's glory – giving him humility and a sense of eternity

The truth doesn't lie

If the enemy cannot destroy us by relentless opposition, he will do the next best thing: he will wage an all-out war on our character. He will undermine our integrity so that people begin to question our sincerity. He will do all in his power to shatter people's confidence and trust in us as individuals. That is why Paul pleads with these young believers in the manner he does. He urges them, appealing to them to accept him as a man, imploring them to accept the message. Actually, what he says is a triple negative.

Paul pulled no punches when he elaborated on point number one; he more or less said, 'Look, the facts are there, the facts are true, the facts speak for themselves!' Basically, what he shared with them in the course of his ministry did *not spring from error*. In other words, he preached the truth of the gospel, the whole truth of the gospel, and nothing but the truth of the gospel. He faithfully preached the Lord Jesus Christ even if it appeared unpalatable to sugary-sermon connoisseurs. He was not a peddler of lies or a purveyor of falsehoods. He was not a scam artist.

The thought behind the Greek word *plane*, translated as *error*, and from which we get our English word, 'planet', is one of movement from one place to another. The word means 'to wander, to roam' like the planets in the ancient sky, not like the stars which behaved more predictably. Error, therefore, is roaming from the truth, it is wandering without any standard, without anything to contain or control us! It is not too difficult to ascertain what they were saying about Paul; we do not have to be rocket scientists to work that one out!

The plain fact is: as a Christian first and a preacher second, he was unflinchingly committed to God's truth. Paul was not deceived, neither was he a deceiver. The gospel that Paul preached was both accurate and authentic.

Modelling the message

Paul was not only dedicated to proclaiming orthodox truth, he was staunchly committed to living the truth. Before one and all, he modelled his message. There were no sensual undertones in what he said or did. There was no *impurity*, for everything he did was open to public scrutiny. He was not guilty of any indiscretions; he was never caught in a position of compromise. There were no sexual connotations contained in his message and no innuendo in his conversation. No matter where he was, or what he did, or who he was with, Paul was above and beyond reproach. No one could point a finger at him!

This is one area where the enemy often attacks the servants of God, and in recent days, there have been many such scandals that have rocked the foundations of not a few organisations. Mind you, it is nothing new, in Paul's day the same was true! In all likelihood, some of Paul's accusers said he was winning converts in return for sexual favours. And the fact that Luke records in Acts 17:4 that a significant number of well-known, well-heeled women were saved only adds fuel to their fire by giving street credibility to their side of the story! If you believe that malarkey, you are as gullible as they come! The truth is: Paul is no filthy dreamer; he is no fornicator hopping in and out of bed with every pretty woman-convert; he is not a man of dubious standards living a double life!

Straight as a die

Paul never attempted to pull the wool over other people's eyes. For him, there was no *attempt to deceive*. There was nothing in his demeanour or conduct that even remotely smacked of the unscrupulous. So far as his evangelistic ministry was concerned, he was not a wolf in sheep's clothing! They had not been lured towards Christ with a false hope. One commentator notes that 'the gospel had not been set out as a decoy to attract potential converts to their own slaughter. Christ was not the bait used to hook the people on some cult.'

There was absolutely nothing devious about his methods. He made no attempt to induce conversions by dangling a juicy carrot in front of people, either by concealing the true cost of discipleship or by offering fraudulent blessings (2 Corinthians 2:17). Mark Howell notes that 'Paul wanted them to know that the gospel was not something to be bartered or bought. It was a gift to be received.'

Here, then, is a threefold claim: Paul insists that his message was true, his motives were pure, and all his methods were open and above board. In each of these his conscience was entirely clear. Paul had no qualms about anything; he had no niggling doubts lurking in the front of his mind, absolutely none! In what he said and in why and how he said it, he was free from anything underhand. These gospel preachers were men of the highest proficiency: men of truth who were true to their Lord, true to their word, true to their calling, and true to their message. Holy and honest men!

2:4

Honour

Paul has a profound feeling of privilege that leaves him stunned and seriously overwhelmed. He sees himself as a custodian entrusted with a priceless and valuable treasure. He was a steward of that which God allocated to him, and we should be too. For example:

- our time – by redeeming it and using it wisely
- our talents – by refusing to bury or hide them under a bushel
- our tithes – by bringing them into the storehouse to be used for the advance of the gospel
- our treasure – by knowing how to effectively handle the word of God

To think that God hand-picked him and counted him worthy to put him into gospel ministry, the sheer thrill of that never left him. He has a great sense of awe and wonder at his calling in life. He says something similar when writing to young Timothy, 'I thank him who has given me strength, Christ Jesus our Lord, because he judged me faithful, appointing me to his service, though formerly I was a blasphemer, persecutor, and insolent opponent. But I received mercy because I had acted ignorantly in unbelief, and the grace of our Lord overflowed for me with the faith and love that are in Christ Jesus' (1 Timothy 1:12-14).

To be *approved by God* is something that left him out of breath. He was spellbound, if not speechless. He passed a rigorous divine selection process having been thoroughly vetted by the Spirit of God. He enjoyed the backing and blessing of the Lord. He was tested times without number and on every occasion he passed with flying colours, because he lived his life for an audience of one.

He knew how to handle himself when disappointment came and John Mark left him for greener pastures (Acts 13:13). He often encountered danger and not infrequently diced with death, e.g. the stoning at Lystra (Acts 14:19). He knew the constant pressure of dealing with internal wrangling and disputes (aka church politics), and came out the other end untainted and untarnished as in the council at Jerusalem (Acts 15:1-29).

Paul had been sorely tried, but here was a man who could be trusted. He had the benefit of God's approval. We cannot get a better commendation than that, for the living Lord Jesus was with him and for him. God endorsed him and gave him a glowing reference. He can face the enemy and walk down the Main Street with his head held high. Come what may, he knows that God has vindicated him and wonderfully blessed his ministry. He is not on an ego trip; he is not flaunting himself; he is not a superstar. He is still Paul, famed for his humility. Just plain Paul, a man whose trust is fixed in God.

The old, old story

What about his preaching? Every word that Paul proclaimed in the course of his spoken ministry he is happy to stand over. There was no other message, no human rhetoric or opinion. The gospel of God's dear Son was the sole foundation upon which the apostle built his exhortations and reproofs.

It was, and still is, the most vital news in the world; at all costs, it must be displayed like a placard to a watching world, shouted to a listening world, and lived out before a world that rarely sees reality. Paul never once got sidetracked by allowing other well-meaning individuals to lead him off the beaten track. For Paul, the main thing was to keep the main thing the main thing! All he related to them from day one was the gospel of the sovereign, saving grace of God. Good enough for him, good enough for me!

God-pleaser

In the early 1990s when President George H W Bush had fiery John Sununu as his Chief of Staff, a reporter asked him if his job was difficult. He quickly answered, 'No.' Thinking he misunderstood the question, he asked him again, and got the same reply. Sununu, a former governor of New Hampshire, then explained why he felt his job was easy: 'I have only one constituent.' He knew his job was to please the President.

Paul has not finished with them yet, for he goes on to affirm that so far as he is concerned, men did not matter, for we read, *so we speak not to please man, but to please God who tests our hearts*. Paul was people-oriented, that is true, but he is definitely not a man-pleaser. He never attempted to play to the gallery and be of all men most plausible. He had no desire, half-hearted or otherwise, to impress them. There was nothing silvery and smooth about his tongue. Herbert B Swope was right when he said, 'I can't give you a sure-fire formula for success, but I can give you a formula for failure: try to please everybody all the time.'

These thoughts come out so clearly in *The Message*, 'We never used words to butter you up. No one knows that better than you. And God knows we never used words as a smoke screen to take advantage of you.' So far as his memory bank can recall, Paul never flattered them on any one occasion. Flattery is a form of callous exploitation. It is like perfume, OK to smell, but not to swallow. Someone defined the difference between flattery and gossip as:

- Flattery is what we say to someone's face which we would never dream of saying behind their back.

- Gossip is what we say behind someone's back which we would never think of saying to their face.

Flattery is telling people what they want to hear so they will do what we want them to do. Flattery is based on the premise that everybody's ego loves to hear good things about themselves. We can look at it like this: if we say a good thing about a person and we have no intent other than to say good about them, that is not flattery; however, if we say a good thing about a person and have in our mind some purpose which will come to our benefit, that equals flattery! It is down to motive, ulterior or otherwise. We read in Proverbs 29:5 that 'a man who flatters his neighbour spreads a net for his feet.' On a similar note, the wisdom of Solomon in Proverbs 26:28 says, 'A lying tongue hates its victims, and a flattering mouth works ruin.'

We all know how it works. Because the average person is so egotistical, the minute someone fires off a volley of nice things about him, his head swells, and in no time at all, he cannot handle the hype. He gets sucked in! That is not communication; quite frankly, it is people manipulation.

I heard about a new pastor who had just preached his first message. The people were coming up to him and saying, 'Wow, that was a wonderful message, it did my heart good.' Finally, a man with a scowl on his face came up and said, 'That's the worst sermon I've ever heard. Who told you that you could preach? If you're a preacher, then I'm the President of the USA.' One of the elders could see that the new pastor was visibly upset so he came over, put his arm around him, and said, 'Don't worry what that man says, he just repeats what everyone else is thinking!'

2:5

The mighty $

Paul came to Thessalonica not for what he could get but for what he could give. That is borne out when he affirms that money did not matter to him, for he writes, *we never came ... with a pretext for greed – God is witness.* Paul was no rip-off merchant out for a quick buck. He never attempted to fleece the flock or meanly exploit them in any way. Even the thought of taking people to the cleaners appalled him. Paul did not have one hand around their shoulder while his other hand was deep in their pocket. Put another way, he and his team did not give the appearance of being poor in order to get rich.

It is a harsh fact of life that, from the beginning, money and ministry have generally appeared to clash. More often than not, they are on a collision course. George MacDonald has wisely observed, 'For every hundred people who can handle failure, there is only one person who can handle success.' Every one of us involved in any aspect of gospel ministry is to be above suspicion in the whole area of finance, for we are accountable to the Lord.

At this point Paul flies in the face of convention and calls on God as his witness. A brave thing for any man to do! But the apostle has no quibbles; Mr Wretched Man That I Am knows he has not let the Lord down in any of these areas. He knows the Lord God is the perfect witness, for he knows everything there is to know since he is omniscient, and unlike fallen man with his prejudices and jaundiced opinions, he cannot lie. Richard Mayhue notes that 'it is impossible for God to perjure himself, thus his witness is the apex in reliability.'

Those of us who preach the gospel of Jesus Christ are not primarily responsible to a church or a mission board, but to the glorified Lord himself, as Head of the church. The local chain of command may tell us where to go and what to do but, ultimately, God is our boss. We are answerable to him as our divine CEO.

There are two sides to this coin: on one side, this is an extremely disconcerting fact because God scrutinises our hearts and its hidden secrets, and his standards are incredibly high – he knows us better than we know ourselves; on the other, it is a marvellously liberating truth since God is a more knowledgeable, impartial, and merciful judge than any human being, or ecclesiastical court, or disciplinary committee will ever be – he knows us better than they know us.

John Stott concludes, 'To be accountable to him is to be delivered from the tyranny of human criticism.' Had Paul not been absolutely sure of his assertions and totally confident of his own position, how foolish it would have been for him to call God as his witness! No matter what we think of Paul, he is not a jackass! I saw a bumper sticker that said, 'If you don't believe in God, I hope you are right!' Make no doubt about it, God will eventually call us all, including Paul, to account.

2:6

No Brownie points

Paul writes with candid openness and razor-sharp honesty, *nor did we seek glory from people, whether from you or from others.* He was not interested in being centre stage; he did not want to hog the limelight. He had no hidden agenda, either for them or himself. He is on the level. This man was the epitome of transparency as he stood before them in all his vulnerability; he was not afraid to confide in them his king-size struggles; he was not ashamed to share with them his many weaknesses. He knew that his humanness was the very avenue through which Christ's work in him would be revealed to them.

Paul knew full well that at any time he could have pulled rank on the Thessalonians. He could even have used his position as an apostle to intimidate and browbeat them into giving him anything he desired. In all fairness, he did not abuse his authority by taking advantage of them. Instead, he came to them as a servant whose ultimate goal was to meet their needs in the best way possible. His was not a mercenary mentality; his tactics were not those of a guerrilla soldier. He was not a shady backstreet character from the underworld, with a hit-and-run mindset. His was not a covert deployment. Certainly not!

This man did not look for esteem or honour; he did not squeeze all the juice from the lemon, for he was no Diotrephes (3 John 9-11). He was not interested in their admiration, nor did he seek their rapturous applause; he did not expect them to show their appreciation in any way or at any time. Paul had a wonderful understanding of human nature and because of that he was not too disappointed if it did not happen. If they showed it, he was immensely thankful and accepted it with a sense of profound gratitude to the Lord.

Even then, he was conscious of his deep indebtedness to the grace of God in his own life, and that kept him on the right side of humility! He had no compulsive desire to be top dog; he did not want to occupy the best seat at the top table; he did not have to be the big shot! Paul never forgot who he was in the eye of God. Here is one gospel preacher who never forgot his roots!

What would Jesus do?

When we take time to analyse Paul's defence, it is abundantly clear that he was not preaching just for the good of his health, nor was he in the Christian ministry to line his own pockets. There was no trace of more-faces-than-Big-Ben hypocrisy in his character and no over-the-top hype in his message. He was not preaching for anything or anyone but Jesus Christ. To him, the Lord was all that mattered. God's verdict was all that counted.

Here is a man who cared supremely what God thought of his ministry. It seems to me that is the reason why Paul is the man he is. When I think of Paul I think of a dear brother who loved the truth and the task in hand. Someone once introduced J Hudson Taylor as a great missionary who had given his life to the Orient because he loved the Chinese. Mr Taylor slowly shook his head and answered thoughtfully,

'No, not because I loved the Chinese, but because I loved God.' Paul passionately embraced the word of the Lord and was totally dedicated to the Lord of the word. It is the 'clean hands and pure heart' syndrome of Psalm 24:4. Perhaps we need to take a long look at ourselves, then pray using the words of Sylvanus Dryden Phelps (1816-95):

Give me a faithful heart,
Likeness to thee,
That each departing day
Henceforth may see
Some work of love begun,
Some deed of kindness done,
Some wanderer sought and won –
Something for thee.

2:7-8

Breaking the mould

A nurse, a servant, and a father are how Paul sees himself in relation to the young church in Thessalonica. In 2:7-12 he develops each of these ideas in a most intriguing way. In that light, this is where good leadership is terrifically important. If this is your forte, your field of expertise, you will know that you can attend many conferences, read a wide variety of books, watch an enormous selection of DVDs and spend hours on YouTube; you can do so much and hear so much, all on the subject of spiritual leadership and how you can be a better leader. A good leader, according to Paul:

- inspires influence – he galvanises people
- seizes the moment – he is up for it
- takes the initiative – he goes for it
- sees the need – he is awake when others are asleep
- delegates responsibility – he shares the load
- ensures the job gets properly done – he does not quit

With the passing of time, many churches lose their vitality. The sparkle goes, the excitement wanes, the thrill evaporates, the shine and lustre fades from their fellowship. Their zing goes ping and their pep goes pop! Instead of allowing God to stretch and shape them into a living, vibrant community of gospel believers, many congregations petrify and mummify into a state of traditionalism. When maintaining status-quo programmes becomes intrinsically more important than ministering to people, the result is an ingrown, inward-looking, stagnant clique. In these few verses, Paul takes the lid off by showing us how we can keep our ministry fresh and alive in Christ. As well as that, Paul gives a few more desirable qualities for those immersed in gospel leadership:

- an ability to feel where people are at (2:7)
- a real heart-affection for people (2:8)
- a kosher lifestyle (2:9-10)
- an eager enthusiasm to hand out bouquets (2:11)
- a genuine gifting to affirm others (2:12)

A mother's touch

The picture is that of a mother and her children where the underlying thought is gentleness. Here we see the tender, loving care Paul showed them in a dignified manner. The use of the word *among* may convey much more than we possibly realise as it suggests that he was in there with them in a heart-and-life involvement.

The word *gentle* comes from a beautiful Greek word, *epios*, used only here and on one other occasion in the New Testament in 2 Timothy 2:24. It simply means to be kind to someone. Paul says in effect: 'As we moved among you, we were kind to you! We did not come to abuse you, or take from you, or exploit you, or ride roughshod over you, or manipulate you; on the contrary, we moved among you with kindness.'

This is a spiritual leader caring for his all-sorts congregation, genuinely concerned about their well-being and sensitive to their personal needs. He accepted them for who they were, he respected them, he extended compassion to them, he displayed a tolerance of their imperfections, he exercised patience in all his dealings with them, and he showed a sense of loyalty to them.

Gentle giant

How gentle is gentle? We do not have to look too far for the answer, for we read at the end of verse 7 that his presence and ministry among them was like *a nursing mother taking care of her own children*. Most of us appreciate that how a mother feeds her young child is almost as important as what she feeds him. We can do so much harm and in the process cause irreparable damage by force-feeding truth down unwilling throats. Thankfully, Paul was not like that! He showed consistent care and compassion appropriate to the needs of those in the church.

Paul was obviously respected as a man of his time, and for better or worse, people tended to take him rather seriously. The average Joe felt inhibited when he was around, he was just so incredibly gifted. He was not the kind of bloke with whom they could crack a joke. They felt jittery with a sense of unease when he was within earshot. That is a shame because they did not have to or need to feel inferior. Paul would be horrified if he thought they felt like that. Because right here, he says, 'we mothered you'. In other words, it was tender love! Soft-hearted love. One translation uses the term 'cherishing' which means 'to warm'. There is no need to scald people with the truth; Paul warmed their hearts, he ignited a spark in their lives.

Bird talk

Another picture is hinted at in Deuteronomy 22:6 where we read of the mother bird covering her young. These young converts were in his arms, ever so close to his heart. Depicted in this snapshot is a mother who cuddles her children, comes down to their level, uses their language, and plays their games; one who becomes childlike with her little ones.

It is a brand of care that is protective and knows just the right moment to step aside. It is not domineering, but is always undergirding. This side of Paul's character does not always shine through in his letters, but we cannot miss it here. It is a bit like the wise words written in the flyleaf of the Bible of the Scottish preacher, John Watson (1850-1907), author of *Beside the Bonnie Brier Bush*, 'Be kind, you don't know what battles people are fighting.'

Such warmth of character shows us the kind of man Paul was in public and behind the scenes. He was not aloof or distant, nor unapproachable. As the Lord's servant, he was never patronising or condescending. He was in there with them, loving them, throwing his arms around them, and that is what he enjoyed most. A devotion that was truly selfless and totally sacrificial. Far from using them to minister to himself, he gave himself to minister to them. Paul was fully aware of their needs and sought to meet them as best he could. A man with a mother's heart! Charles Swindoll makes the interesting point that 'the pulpit shouldn't be a stainless steel milk dispenser but a rocking chair where the pastor lovingly nurses the church.'

A mother's love

Paul develops his argument further when he unfolds the role of a mother in the full beauty of its metaphorical meaning. Here we see a real mother in her true colours when he writes, *so, being affectionately desirous of you, we were ready to share with you not only the gospel of God but also our own selves, because you had become very dear to us.* No matter how cynical we may be about Paul's approach to gospel ministry, or how critical we may be of his attitude to these young believers, these selected words from verse 8 speak volumes, for here is affection at its finest and best. Paul yearned for them with a big heart, just like a young mother hankering after her child. It is like a mother being irresistibly drawn to her child, so powerfully strong is the emotional pull. When Paul looked at his spiritual children in the crèche in Thessalonica, there was a bond, a heart connection, between them. They were his pride and joy.

It is hugely significant that Paul did not turn them over to babysitters or childminders, choosing instead to care for them and look after them himself. He felt so deeply for them because they genuinely won his heart. Please do not get the idea from Paul's loving language that he was a spiritual softie! As a warrior for the gospel he had a tough exterior and a soft inside! Paul had enough spiritual perception to distinguish between the real enemy and those who were hurting and lost in darkness. He knew they were imperfect like himself, and because they often suffered from the dreaded collywobbles, they regularly needed a helping, supportive hand along life's way.

A pastor is not one who lobs instructions from the trenches like hand grenades to those struggling in the game of life. Paul did not bark commands at them like a sergeant major on a military parade ground. It is not the classic scenario of them and us, sitting on opposite sides of the same room, waiting for someone to carry out the necessary introductions. A warm relationship like this, within the family of God, is one that cannot be carried out at arm's length. Hence the need to be like Paul, and be in there with them!

He was more than happy to share the gospel with them, but surpassing that, he was willing to wrap his life up in theirs. He was so motivated and constrained by love that nothing was too much trouble to him. He gave everything, holding nothing back, in unreserved abandonment; he was one hundred and ten percent committed to them. Paul was more than just a put-your-coin-in vending machine. He did not only dispense biblical truth, he actually imparted his life to them, for he valued them; he acknowledged their worth before God and he appreciated their worth in his own life. He stayed with them and fleshed out the gospel that he preached. His whole life incarnated the love of God. The nineteenth-century British Prime Minister Benjamin Disraeli (1804-81) noted that 'the greatest good you can do for another is not just to share your riches, but to reveal to him his own.'

2:9

Tentmaker

For you remember, brothers, our labour and toil: we worked night and day, that we might not be a burden to any of you, while we proclaimed to you the gospel of God. It is apparent that Paul knew exactly what he was doing and it shows itself in many different ways. Paul got it absolutely right from at least three angles – his preaching, his priorities, and his profession.

His preaching is spot on. The only message Paul shared with them is what he calls *the gospel of God*. In short: the good news, the best news, the only news worth listening to, aka the evangel. Such a message incorporated three fundamental truths: Christ died for our sins, was buried, and raised again on the third day (1 Corinthians 15:3-4). It was, therefore, solidly biblical. If we had been there, sitting on hard wooden benches alongside the worshippers in Thessalonica, we would have heard the clear, consistent declaration of God's word, a gospel message pregnant with truth. We would be spared the agony of listening to the idle ramblings and whimsical opinions of a preacher man.

His priorities were also right. Paul did not want to be a financial burden to them so he plied his arduous trade as a tentmaker by day, and when the sun was down, he preached the gospel by night. Paul did not arrive in town as a gospel virtuoso and demand celebrity treatment. He was not like Diotrephes (3 John 9), or the Pharisees (Matthew 23:4), or Simon Magus (Acts 8:9-24), all of whom acted like pastoral prima donnas. Instead, he was tireless in his efforts as he expended monumental amounts of energy, working himself to the bone.

It was a really hard struggle at times with many litres of tears shed, but he did it all for them. It was not an easy option; this was no cheap alternative lifestyle. Paul did not adopt the attitude that said, 'Stop the world, I want to get off!' All of this is an unmistakable indication that his priorities were on target. Paul knows that what he is doing is right, so he gets on with it; he knows where he is going, and he gets there. Oswald Chambers (1874-1917) makes the point, 'If we are going to be used by God, he will take us through a multitude of experiences that are not meant for us at all; they are meant to make us useful in his hands.'

2:10

Right profession

You are witnesses, and God also, how holy and righteous and blameless was our conduct toward you believers. Paul is a brave man. What a staggering claim for any mortal man to make! He says they know it. That is fine, we have no qualms about that; but Paul does not leave it there, he takes a breath, leaps forward and says, God knows it. He is a man of unquestioned probity as he tells them how it was when he was privileged to be with them.

- He is holy – his conduct in relation to God.

He is a man of piety. When we look at Paul we see something beautifully attractive about his demeanour. There is a warm glow to his personality that only comes when a person is walking close with the Lord. He and Jesus are on the same wavelength, in touch and in tune with one another. So much so that God's name, God's will, and God's kingdom were his priority (Matthew 6:9-10). We see someone who knows to whom he belongs and is, therefore, perfectly satisfied. He was single-minded in that he was sold out to Jesus. His all is on the altar, he kept nothing back for himself.

- He is righteous – his conduct in relation to his fellow man.

He is a just man who behaved himself in such a manner that his whole life was beyond reproach. He did not leave himself open for criticism; he was upright in all aspects of public ministry. No man could point a finger at him. They would try and have a go, but they were on a hiding to nothing. There were no chinks in the armour of his character. No matter where he was or who he was with, he was kosher in all his dealings.

From Paul's vantage point, nothing was conducted under the counter; no business was done behind closed doors in clandestine hush-hush meetings. Before other people his life was an open book. He had no hidden agenda for plugging his latest autographed epistle, or touting his success as a church planter, or begging for money to keep his ministry alive.

- He is blameless – his conduct in relation to self.

We all know that Paul was not sinless, but he was blameless. We are very much aware of the fact that he was not perfect; he had his faults – plenty of them – like the rest of us. He never said he was any different! In our misplaced enthusiasm to applaud our boyhood hero, we have lifted him to a level that is much more than he ever aspired to. We have put a halo on his head, given him celebrity status, and hung a 'Do not touch!' notice around his highly polished neck.

Paul was no pin-up or cultic personality. A boringly ordinary man, he was open, honest, and transparent, with no airs or graces. In public: blameless. In private: blameless. This peripatetic preacher is a man of renowned rectitude. If he said he would do it, he did it. He kept his promises. He never scampered into the shadows when the light was switched on. He did what was right even when no one else was looking and he did what was right even when others were compromising all around him.

Martin Luther King Jr. (1929-68) observed that 'the ultimate measure of a man is not where he stands in moments of comfort and convenience, but where he stands at times of challenge and controversy.'

For Paul, old-fashioned decency was not just a convenient prop or something for him to lean on when he needed a character reference; it was something that came from deep within. It did not fade or fluctuate with the passing of time or depend on the company it was in. It remained intact whether the test was the worst of times in adversity or the best of times in prosperity.

When we think of what happened to Paul in a miscellany of situations, it is good to realise that here is a guy who walked away unscathed in terms of personal uprightness. Some people in today's world are so twisted they could hide behind a corkscrew. Not Paul, he is as straight as a gun barrel! Winning or losing, passing or failing, his integrity shone through.

2:11-12

Paternal instincts

We have a beautiful picture emerging when Paul's relationship is likened to that of a father with his children. John MacArthur says of the apostle at this point, 'Paul acted like a man. There was a side of him that acted like a mother but there was another side of him that acted like a man, like a father with strength and courage. And he never flinched from the immeasurable risks of life and the challenges that he faced because one, he was assured of God's presence; two, he knew the cause was just; and three, he trusted an unfailing sovereignty.'

Paul had a definite paternal instinct that ensured each person received the best, individual attention. Each one was vitally important to him. They mattered. What did he do? He modelled the message before them. But he did a lot more, for it goes beyond pattern to precept.

- He *encouraged* them.

He lifted their hearts. He picked them up when they were on a real downer. People get discouraged so easily, so his ministry was one of reassuring, ongoing support. He gave them the priceless gifts of a listening ear and an understanding heart. He came alongside them and made them feel so much better. It is the Barnabas factor worked out in the context of a local church family. He excelled in motivation.

- He *comforted* them.

He certainly did not pamper or mollycoddle them. Because of his unique style in ministering into their situation, he made them want to do better in themselves. He counselled them to keep on trying, to hang in there, to hold on tight. He sought to bring out the best in them, while others with the gift of agitation often bring out the worst in us.

- He *urged* them.

He testified to them from his own experience; it is the empathy principle established by Paul in 2 Corinthians 1:3-4 being put into practice. He shared with them what happened to him. He followed the shining example of the prophet when he sat where they sat (Ezekiel 3:15). Remember Corrie Ten Boom? When her dear sister Betsy was dying amidst the unthinkable horrors of Ravensbrück concentration camp, she uttered a sentence that has travelled all around the world. She said, 'There is no pit so deep that Christ is not deeper still.' Another profound statement of equal worth came from her lips when she said, 'They will listen to us because we've been here.' This is so true, because God has no problems, he only has plans.

The modern-day hymn writer Stuart Townend summed it up with these words:

There is a hope that lifts my weary head,
A consolation strong against despair,

That when the world has plunged me in its deepest pit,
I find the Saviour there!

Paul could identify with them. He could relate to them. That is why he *urged* them. It is as plain and simple as that! Here is a pastoral leader with his sleeves rolled up, leading by example and encouragement; a man with the ability to carry out a good resolution long after the excitement of the moment has passed.

Being what God wants us to be

Why did Paul do it? What was his ultimate goal? It was, as he says himself, so that they might *walk in a manner worthy of God*. Here is the big difference between the mother and father traits in Paul. The 'mother side' wants to provide what is needed at a given moment; the 'father side' wants to produce the product at the end: a delicate balance that needs to be maintained. 'Mama' Paul wants to cherish, nurture, love, hold, and affirm. Perfectly natural, for that is the motherly instinct coming to the fore. Then 'Papa' Paul comes along and says, 'That's all very well, in fact, it's wonderful; but we want to be sure at the end that he's living according to God's standards.'

Both – mother and father – complement each other beautifully. It is all about modelling, mentoring, motivating, and then moving them on to the next step. That is where the involvement of a father is mega important, for any father worth his salt wants each of his children to walk in a manner worthy of the God who has called them. And that is what they needed to do: they needed to learn how to walk.

In those early stages of finding their spiritual feet, Paul was constantly available to them as a father. He was at their beck and call. The importance of this experience is underlined with the reminder that the Lord is the one *who calls you*. That phrase is in the present tense. They have been called to salvation. Now God is calling them to a life of obedience and holiness.

Whether we preach from a pulpit on Sunday morning or sit behind a computer monitor or stand in front of a kitchen sink on Monday morning, God wants to blend our vocation with our calling. Your vocation is special, your calling is sacred, regardless of whether you wear a clerical collar, a blue collar, a white collar, or no collar at all. No matter what job pays your household bills at the end of the month, he wants you to come to terms with your calling and use your 9-to-5, Monday-thru-Friday berth to further his kingdom. Down here we are an integral part of his kingdom. One day we shall leave this world behind when we enter his eternal kingdom and share his glory forever. What a day that will be!

These are the bones of godly leadership – intelligent gospel leadership by God's design – it is giving people hope. Napoleon noted that 'a leader is a dealer in hope.' On one hand, a concern for the whole person; on the other, a concern for the process. On one hand, a concern for kindness; on the other, a concern for control. On one hand, a concern for affection; on the other, a concern for authority. On one hand, embracing; on the other, exhorting. On one hand, cherishing; on the other, challenging. Where there is that healthy and proper balance, God can work in a glorious way in our lives. If we have a generous mix and match of all these components, we have the makings of a biblical leader, a gospel leader who stands head and shoulders above everyone else. In fact, we have a Paul, and because we have a Paul, we have a church in Thessalonica. That proves the point!

Our friend Paul fulfilled that role admirably for he was a leader and a servant at the same time. Servant leadership. A businessman once asked Lorne Sanny (1920-2005), former president of Navigators, how he would know when he had a servant attitude. Sanny told him, 'By how you act when you're treated like one.' The words of Graham Kendrick's song, *The Servant King*, spring to mind, for they say it so well and come as a fresh challenge:

So let us learn how to serve,
And in our lives enthrone him,
Each other's needs to prefer,
For it is Christ we're serving.

2:13

Growing pains

Growing pains can be a problem! An understatement? When we look at the final verses in the chapter, there is copious evidence to suggest that these relatively young believers were going through something similar. They are stretching, developing, maturing, and growing; and for all of us who have been there and done that, we know there are times when it can be horrendously painful. They faced so many trials and so much trouble. They suffered. Their only crime was their sincere love for the Lord Jesus. When we stand back and look objectively at their situation and try to analyse what was happening, one inescapable fact emerges: it was tough living for Jesus in the first century.

Paul chose his words carefully as he summed up their egregious predicament. He says they have *suffered*, which is the same word that is used for the sufferings of Jesus. He then says they *drove us out*, which means to be rejected by those to whom you seek to minister. Another word employed is *oppose*, which is used of chilling winds that blow against us. Then he says they were *hindered*, which pictures a road so broken that travel is virtually impossible. Welcome to the real world! This was life as it really was. Life in the raw.

Paul was an extremely worried man. He was deeply concerned about their welfare: would they make it through another day? Yet, like them, he similarly displays a real joy in his life. No matter how adverse the circumstances, or on which front the enemy is attacking, the Lord is always with us. He goes through it with us. We are not on our own. Paul shows them three resources they have and on which they can depend when life is lived in the relentless environment of a pressure cooker.

- We have the faith – God's word in us.
- We have the family – God's people around us.
- We have a future – God's glory before us.

A right attitude

Paul thanks the Lord for them because of their splendid attitude to the precious word of God. Clement Stone (1902-2002) makes the point that 'there is little difference in people, but that little difference makes a big difference. The little difference is attitude. The big difference is whether it is positive or negative.' Paul says, *And we also thank God constantly for this, that when you received the word of God, which you heard from us, you accepted it not as the word of men but as what it really is, the word of God, which is at work in you believers.*

That means they accepted it not as the word of men, but as it is, the oracles of God. It is the living word of a God who is alive; a message unchanged and unchanging, timeless truth which is never dated. The word of God is God's word to us. The 16th President of the USA, Abraham Lincoln (1809-65), noted that 'the Bible is the best gift God has ever given to man.'

When we read the Bible for ourselves we quickly discover that it speaks to the major issues facing every generation. A good working knowledge of Scripture is the master key to understanding the vital problems of our day. Back then, how did they see it?

Appreciation

They knew it was so much more than the words of mortal men. Far from viewing it as some concoction of his own, they had no doubts in their minds that they heard the word of God every time Paul opened his mouth. His message was not only a message *from* God, it was also a message *about* God. On that note, J I Packer, author of *Evangelism and the Sovereignty of God*, says that, 'In preaching, the word of God delivers through the preacher a message from God to his people about God and godliness.'

Their enthusiastic and positively open-hearted reception of the word of God gives us an insight into what made Paul tick as an apostle of Jesus Christ. His language is strangely reminiscent of the Old Testament prophets who would often preface their message by saying, 'The word of the Lord came to me' (Jeremiah 1:4) or 'Thus says the Lord' (Isaiah 48:17). This goes a long way to explaining Paul's dogged persistence in the face of massive odds. He always believed it was much too soon to quit. He was not a self-publicist peddling pet notions of his own. If that had been the case, persecution would have knocked the conceit out of him long before he ever reached Macedonia.

He was a spokesman for the Almighty, a herald with the king's message and the king's commission. Mark Howell writes, 'What a preacher believes about the Bible will determine how he preaches the Bible, and how he preaches the Bible will influence how his church responds to what the Bible says.' On a similar note, John MacArthur said that 'the preacher is not a chef; he's a waiter. God doesn't want you to make the meal; he just wants you to deliver it to the table without messing it up.'

So when Paul started to speak, people sat up and listened. They were riveted to the spot. They took notice. We often contrast words and actions as though words are empty, worthless things that compare badly with deeds. On one hand, some people are all talk, while others get things done! On the other hand, what Paul said as he declared the whole counsel of God was a force to be reckoned with. It produced results. It bore fruit.

These dear friends whose lives were radically changed, passionately believed it to be the living word of the living Lord. The Bible is not like any other book. It stands alone and above all other volumes and weighty tomes found in every library throughout the world. It is significantly different in origin, character, and content. The Bible is the word of God, inspired by the Spirit of God, for all the people of God. When we hear it or read it we are receiving his message, listening to his voice, and considering his thoughts.

What is our attitude to God's word right now? Do we treasure it like Job who reckoned it was worth more than his daily steak sandwich (Job 23:12), or like David who said it was of more value than money and even 'more to be desired than fine gold' (Psalm 19:10)? They appreciated it!

Appropriation

Paul used two words which combine to show their intelligent response to the proclamation of biblical truth. The first is *received*, and the second is *accepted*. The first means 'to accept it from another'. The second means 'to welcome it warmly'. One has the idea of hearing with the ear; the other implies a hearing of the heart. They not only heard the word but they took it and made it part and parcel of their lives.

They assimilated the truth, personalised the truth, and they did it to such an extent that it became an integral part of their spiritual makeup. The word of life became a way of life to them! As the old preacher was heard to say, 'They went through the Book and the Book went through them.' It penetrated down deep into the inner sanctum of their lives. They got the message, and the message got them!

We can look at it from a slightly different angle when we borrow the analogy from a parable; because of their upbeat response, we are able to affirm that the living seed was planted in the exceptionally fertile soil of willing, responsive hearts. When Jesus communicated with his followers, he often focused attention on their attitude to the word of his Father. In three different Gospels:

- 'He who has ears *let* him hear' (Matthew 13:9).
- 'Consider carefully *what* you hear' (Mark 4:24).
- 'Consider carefully *how* you listen' (Luke 8:18).

The time has come when we need to learn again the profitable art of meditation, chewing the cud of Scripture. The Puritan preacher Thomas Manton (1620-77) said, 'We should always be chewing and sucking out the sweetness of this cud.' Meditation is to spiritual life what digestion is to physical life. If we did not properly digest our recommended daily intake of food, eventually we would die. According to Thomas Watson (1620-86), 'A Christian without meditation is like a soldier without weapons, or a workman without tools.' It takes time to meditate, but it is the best way I know to appropriate the teaching of Scripture and thereby grow in our relationship with the Lord. It has nothing to do with getting sound-bites from the Lord. It is not the mentality that says, 'Lord, speak to me, you have sixty seconds, starting now!'

There is an awful lot to be said for quietly waiting upon the Lord as we ponder his message to our hearts. We should approach our daily portion of Scripture with an intense longing to hear God speak to our hearts and minds. And when he does address us, we should take time to let it sink in, allowing it to soak our hearts and flow through our spiritual veins. We then become a people saturated with truth, permeated with the word of God. The reality of Christ suffuses our lives so deeply and so completely that it changes the very chemistry of our being. It was C H Spurgeon who said in his inimitable way, 'A Bible which is falling apart usually belongs to someone who is not.'

Application

So far as these young believers were concerned, they had no problems in this respect. They not only appreciated and appropriated gospel truth, they went one step further and applied it. In other words, they put it into practice. They knew that between saying and doing, many a good pair of shoes is worn out. Good listeners! Good livers!

They were doers of the word (James 1:25) and that is where real spiritual blessing is found. Therein lies the age-old secret, it is all about living it out in the peaks and troughs of everyday life. In the comfort of our home, in college lecture hall or university campus, at the supermarket checkout with a week's groceries in the trolley, standing in the bus line when the rain is lashing down, in the world of business, down on the factory floor, wherever we are, whoever we are, it is all about living out the word of God.

God's word changes people, and if we let it, it will change us too (1 Peter 1:23). 'With the heart we appreciate the word of God, with the mind we appropriate the word of God, and with the will we apply the word of God,' notes Warren Wiersbe. When the whole person is controlled by the word, we evolve into men and women of the word.

2:14-16

The enemy fights back

When trouble knocks at our front door, how do we handle it? If we are scrupulously honest, when the enemy strikes, sometimes we go down and under, or we cave in and collapse under the intensity of relentless pressure, or we feel hurt and badly let down, or we feel particularly vulnerable and isolated. At times we are prone to feel as though we are very much on our own and that we are the only ones going through a rough patch. The abiding fact remains and it cannot be emphasised enough, we are not!

For you, brothers, became imitators of the churches of God in Christ Jesus that are in Judea. For you suffered the same things from your own countrymen as they did from the Jews, who killed both the Lord Jesus and the prophets, and drove us out, and displease God and oppose all mankind by hindering us from speaking to the Gentiles that they might be saved – so as always to fill up the measure of their sins. But wrath has come upon them at last!

Paul's words are less than complimentary. They amount to sober reality. In the cold light of a new day they are a substantiated fact of life. The harrowing and traumatising experiences of all those in Thessalonica was more or less a carbon copy of what was happening to those believers further east in the environs of Judea.

Samuel Johnson (1709-84), famous literary giant of the eighteenth century once said, 'I never think I have hit hard unless it rebounds.' In the same way, the antagonism that the early believers faced was an indisputable proof of the transformational power of the gospel in their lives. Christianity made a massive enough difference so as to leave their contemporaries well and truly rattled. There was nothing strange or sinister about their misfortune. In fact, it was to be expected. Sooner or later it was bound to happen. In a providential sense, they were destined for it. The Christian life is no manicured bed of perfumed roses. It is not all plain sailing on a calm sea into an orange sunset, they quickly discovered that. They would be stronger and better for it at the end of the day.

Facing tough times together

They were only human, with roller-coaster feelings, but they were definitely not on their own. That is one of the great values of being part of God's international community. We stand together in our darkest hours. When dark clouds surround us, we cling to the Lord and hold on to one another. In the family of God, we should be able to find in each other a measure of help and encouragement. A touch of empathy. They were stressed-out, but they were strengthened!

It was when Elijah isolated himself from the others that his heart sank to an all-time low and he wanted to quit (1 Kings 19:3-14). The lesson is: lonely saints are easy meat for the enemy. We may be saved by grace alone through faith alone, but God never intended for us to live life alone. Whether we realise it or not, we desperately need each other. We cannot go it alone. In the battles of life, in the changing vicissitudes of life, in the mixed fortunes of life, in all the comings and goings of life, we can survive if we stay together.

Who killed Jesus?

Paul does not beat about the bush when he points an accusing finger at the Jews for their fiercely hostile attitude to the Lord Jesus. It is worth noting that some Bible teachers have argued that Paul's language in these verses betrays a spiteful streak that was unworthy of him. It has even been suggested that he was in a stinkingly bad mood because of his treatment at the hands of Jews in Corinth. Let us remember – and this is important – Paul was a Jewish man himself and he had every reason to be justifiably proud of his heritage and upbringing (Philippians 3:4-6); he avidly yearned to see his own people, the sons and daughters of Abraham, won to saving faith in Yeshua Hamashiach (Romans 10:1); he even said on one memorable occasion that he would willingly contemplate the loss of his personal salvation if that would act as a catalyst to bring theirs about (Romans 9:1-5).

Paul was a man of high moral principles and remarkable intelligence and gifting. Those qualities did not cloud or colour his thinking, or dull his mental capacity or deaden his critical faculties; in fact, the opposite is probably the case. He was alert to all that was going on; he did not stand with his tail in the air and his head buried ostrich-like in the sand. So when a scribe picks up his quill and writes on the parchment on Paul's behalf, there is a reason for it. It is not what they necessarily wanted to hear, but it had to be said nonetheless.

This is no charm offensive when he writes in the scathing manner he does. He explicitly says, in a matter-of-fact kind of way, you *killed the Lord Jesus*. In a politically correct era when such grave matters are regarded as highly sensitive, that could be regarded as a reprehensible, anti-Semitic statement. But like so much in Scripture, there is a lot more to it than first meets the eye. It is also true to say that the Romans were implicated in the death of Jesus.

The one will-not-go-away fact is: so were all of us, as it was for our sin that he died. Your sin. My sin. Indeed, Paul included himself personally in this (Galatians 2:20); he never forgot that he had once been a blasphemer and a persecutor (1 Timothy 1:13). Nevertheless, the Jewish people as a whole shared the blame and said so in Matthew 27:25. While implicating ourselves, we cannot exonerate them!

On the charge sheet

The second charge Paul directed at them is that they *killed the prophets*. He was not the first to do this, for Jesus himself accused them (Matthew 23:29-31; *cf.* Luke 13:34). The third charge levelled against them is that they *also drove us out*, which seems to put the apostles on a par with the prophets (1 Corinthians 4:9). Number four is when Paul draws attention to the fact that *they displease God*, especially by rejecting his Messiah. The last one is when he says they *oppose all mankind*. This phrase brings to mind the famous saying of Tacitus when he described them thus, 'Towards all other people (i.e. except their fellow Jews) they feel only hatred and hostility.'

Gagging God

Paul added fuel to the fire in verse 16 when he explained their hostility to the human race in terms of their attempt to stop the apostles preaching the gospel. Like Jonah before them, they did not want the Gentiles to be saved! An echo of this less-than-friendly attitude is found back in Matthew 23:13. Paul saw this policy for what it really was: appalling. The Jews savagely killed the Lord Jesus and ruthlessly persecuted the prophets and apostles; they were also obstructing the spread of the gospel, thereby hindering the work of salvation. They attempted to silence God's spokesmen.

What could be more distasteful and horrible than withholding a life-saving message from dying men? It was God's express will and desire that all men be saved through the gospel of Christ, but the Jews wanted no one to find salvation in Jesus, even though he specifically came to save them from their sin. In effect, they did not like what they saw or heard, so they resorted to the old tactic of attempting to gag the living God.

Payday coming

Paul gives it to them straight from the shoulder. He could not have spelt it out any clearer. What a serious indictment to make against any people group! It is enough to cause them to shudder in their boots and shake like leaves on a windy autumn day. As a direct consequence of their crass arrogance and blatant antagonism, they sinned at the most severe level, so much so that their cup of transgression and guilt was filled to the brim with their heinous and despicable sins. The God who acted before is the same holy God who will not hesitate to act a second time! Just as God's judgment fell on the Amorites when their sin 'reached its full measure', so it would fall on the Jewish people when they had filled up the measure of their sins and those of their forefathers (Genesis 15:16; *cf.* Matthew 23:32).

Someone has ruefully said, 'Nothing could do this more directly or fully than persecuting the preachers of the gospel.' God does not sit idly by while men try to outwit and pull a quick one over him; he does not stand back and act as if nothing has ever happened. Truth be told, they get their comeuppance, for Paul says *wrath has come upon them at last*. Reading a statement of intent like that sends shivers down the spine and we break out into a cold sweat. This refers to God's eternal wrath in exactly the same way as John spoke of it (John 3:18). One where the outcome is so certain, it is guaranteed. There is no last-minute reprieve letting them off the hook.

According to 1:10, God's wrath is future, but here it appears to be past. The use of the words *has come* is clearly indicative of the fact that, so far as God is concerned, the whole judgment scenario has already happened (*cf.* Romans 8:30 for a similar use of this tense). Basically, it conveys the sober and solemn idea, as outlined by J B Phillips, that 'the wrath of God is over their heads.' Richard Mayhue, in his fine commentary, has this to say by way of summary, 'Those who reject the gospel or refuse to let it be preached will know the eternal wrath of God to the extreme, while those who believe the gospel will be rescued altogether from experiencing God's wrath.'

2:17-18

Tangled emotions

In these last few verses, Paul gives the inside story of his tangled emotions. I am just so glad that Paul is so honest. There were times when he was scared stiff and other occasions when he bubbled with joy. I sometimes wonder where the misguided idea ever arose that Paul was a stern, cold individual. We cannot read this letter without sensing the genuine warmth of his heart and the voluminous depth of his love. At time of writing, Paul was ministering alone in promiscuous Corinth, where he felt the incredible loneliness of that moment. His mind was working overtime as he thought about his very dear friends further north in Thessalonica. It had given Paul no pleasure leaving the city, he had not departed voluntarily. On the contrary, he had been dragged out of the place kicking and screaming.

Paul was not in the least ashamed to admit that he loved these folk, they meant so much to him. He felt a sense of bereavement because he could not be with them. His heart was with them and he wanted his body to return to where his heart was. He felt deprived because he did not have a chance to say a proper goodbye, so he longed to return. These words from Paul were not just for a good day. This was the passion in his heart every day.

Listen to his pastoral concern for the Philippians: 'It is right for me to feel this way about you all, because I hold you in my heart, for you are all partakers with me of grace, both in my imprisonment and in the defence and confirmation of the gospel. For God is my witness, how I yearn for you all with the affection of Christ Jesus' (1:7-8).

From his perspective, he was on the receiving end of an enforced raw deal, the rough end of the stick. It was a brutal experience and not one that he would have chosen in the normal course of events. He felt like an orphan, as he hinted quite openly by using the words *torn away from you*. He felt bereft. It speaks of an unnatural kind of separation, both forcible and extremely painful. Perhaps a better translation would be 'kidnapped'. When Paul left the gospel community in Thessalonica, he felt shanghaied.

Between a rock and a hard place

It was an unbelievably difficult experience for him and it must have had a distressing influence on them; if it was traumatic for him, it must have been unthinkably tough for them. Paul desperately wanted to stay and minister to them but the enemy drove him out. Events were outside his control and there was nothing he could do about them. He tried to return, but again and again, his path was solidly blocked, there was just no way through. Humanly speaking, it was impossible!

There were many obstacles strewn across the road and Satan effectively stopped him from making any headway. Some of the translations prefer to use the word *hindered* in this context. Such a word is used in a military sense of breaking up or cluttering up a road so as to make it impassable to the opposing army. So far as Paul was concerned, this was intense spiritual warfare and the enemy was lying in ambush to attack him. He was in serious danger of being caught in the crossfire. Paul lays the blame fairly and squarely at the devil's door when he says that he is the one responsible for thwarting his valiant and persistent attempts to make contact with them.

There have been many opinions offered as to the precise reason for this minor inconvenience, a hiccup in Paul's well-laid plans, a blip on his travel schedule. At the end of the day, the reason why is down to pure conjecture on our part; the indisputable fact is that it happened and that was that! It has been well said, 'When God is at work, Satan is surely alongside.' What Christ was building in terms of the church, the devil was committed to destroying. It is not surprising then to see Satan so visible and with such a high profile in so many local churches in the New Testament.

Satan is alive and well

A quick look at Scripture indicates that Satan's chief activity and goal in our lives is twofold: he will do all in his power to get us to think differently to gospel truth and, consequently, to act disobediently to God's will. He attempts to accomplish this end through four basic strategies:

- by twisting the truth of God's word (Matthew 4:1-11)

- by tarnishing the testimony of God's people (Acts 5:1-11)

- by trashing a believer's zeal to accomplish God's work (2 Corinthians 12:7-10)

- by thinning down the effectiveness of God's church (Acts 22:3-5)

Those are four effective pincer movements on the part of the devil! The encouraging fact is that Paul was able to discern between God closing a door to ministry and Satan blocking the way. That is true, but it still leaves one question lurking in the front of our minds: How can we explain such a terribly frustrating incident? There is only one possible explanation: the overruling providence of the Lord. As Philip Arthur writes, 'Although his movements are circumscribed by the sovereign purposes of God, Satan has an objective reality and is permitted, in measure, to hamper the servants of God.' The Lord sees tomorrow; we only see today. Our disappointments are his appointments. Our lives unfold, open and close, according to his plan.

A pupil in God's school of hard knocks

It goes without saying that God had something better, much better, for him; there was something around the next curve on life's road that he could not yet see. We need to always remind ourselves that God permits Satanic opposition. An obvious example is the moving story of Job, a man who lost everything: his family, his home, and his health. But God allowed it to happen. It was true of Job and it is certainly true of Paul that God gave the go-ahead for this to take place, but he ultimately used it to bring Paul closer to himself.

Paul learned a whole range of vital lessons through this traumatic and devastating experience. God in his wisdom used this distressing episode to teach Paul some unforgettable lessons in the school of life, which he probably could not learn any other way. So what did he do? He did not look back and pine and give in to guilt feelings of regret and remorse. Rather, he looked forward with anticipation; he looked ahead with a keen sense of expectancy in his heart, and rejoiced. Paul is not deterred, he is not put off. The thought of throwing the towel into the ring does not even enter his mind.

2:19-20

Tomorrow's world

He has a joyful hope that is undiminished by the seemingly insurmountable and immovable problems that he is wrestling with. He scanned the distant horizon and saw his dear friends from Thessalonica in the intimate presence of his Lord in heaven. One writer says, 'In a sudden burst of energy, Paul breaks out in hallelujahs over the Thessalonians. To demonstrate the ultimate in commitment and love, Paul asks one question in three parts.' *For what is our hope or joy or crown of boasting before our Lord Jesus at his coming? Is it not you?* And then Paul gives us the answer we have all been waiting for when he affirms, *For you are our glory and joy.*

Moffat's Law

Robert Moffat (1795-1883), Scottish missionary to Southern Africa, when asked to sign a young woman's autograph book, wrote the following:

> *My album is a savage breast*
> *Where tempests brood and shadows rest*

Without one ray of light.
To write the name of Jesus there
And see that savage bow in prayer
And point to worlds more bright and fair,
This is my soul's delight.

Moffat does not anticipate a crown for his work with them; they are his crown!

We'll meet again

I think most of us realise that Paul had many spiritual hopes which were all bound up in the will of the God of hope (Romans 15:13). In one way or another all these hopes relate to the believer's progress towards our ultimate salvation of being with the Lord. For example, Paul hoped in:

- the glory of God (Romans 5:2)
- righteousness (Galatians 5:5)
- salvation (Colossians 1:5)
- Jesus Christ (1 Timothy 1:1)
- eternal life (Titus 3:7)
- the second coming of Christ (Titus 2:13)

But right here, Paul's hope is specifically focused on God's unexcelled work in their lives. He and others paid a price personally for their spiritual progress and he had high hopes that one day salvation's work would be completed in a final sense.

They brightened his day

They were a source of unparalleled joy to Paul and his colleagues. In fact, Paul is singing from the same song sheet as John when he writes in his tiny third epistle that he found no greater joy than seeing his children walk in truth (3 John 4). Paul speaks of the believers in Philippi in much the same way (Philippians 4:1). He often found occasion to rejoice in the Lord (1 Corinthians 1:31); he revelled and rejoiced in the hope of the glory of God (Romans 5:2); there was never a day went by when he did not rejoice with a sense of profound gratitude for the cross of Christ (Galatians 6:14); and he often rejoiced in the lives of those to whom he had the rare privilege of ministering (2 Thessalonians 1:4; *cf.* 2 Corinthians 9:2).

To crown it all

They not only brought unsurpassed joy into his life, he also sees them as his crown! This crown is not the royal diadem of Revelation 19:12 which is reserved for the head of the sovereign Lord Jesus, the King of kings. It is more like the simple garland or wreath worn by the victor as the top prize in some athletic contest, the equivalent of winning a gold medal in the Olympic games of the modern era.

The Greek word *stephanos* indicates various aspects of our so great salvation. A concordance will show that there are five key references to this crown in the Bible: one, the imperishable wreath that celebrates salvation's victory over corruption (1 Corinthians 9:25); two, the righteous wreath that celebrates salvation's victory over unrighteousness

(2 Timothy 4:8); three, the unfading wreath of glory that celebrates salvation's victory over defilement (1 Peter 5:4); four, the wreath of life that celebrates salvation's victory over death (James 1:12; *cf.* Revelation 2:10); and, five, the wreath of exultation which celebrates salvation's victory over every kind of persecution of believers (1 Thessalonians 2:19-20).

Seeing events through the lens of eternity

What a breathtakingly beautiful vision the Lord in his tender love and grace gave to Paul. It was just what he needed, it changed his outlook, giving him a new perspective on life in the here and now, because he caught a glimpse of the there and then. Troubles and trials will come; they are par for the course for every one of us who love the Lord. In such moments we need to take a long view of things. We need to view them from the vantage point of a higher throne in heaven. That is how Paul lived; and died.

He wanted to shape tomorrow, so he started today. He planned not for the short term, but the longer term. Paul mapped out clear goals for himself and his ministry and he went for them one by one. Obviously, all these activities were subject to the overruling will of God in his life; nevertheless, Paul's actions today were governed by what God may do tomorrow.

In spite of what some of them were saying about him in the church at Thessalonica, he knew that one day Christ would return to reward him. That is what kept him going, it was all the incentive he needed. The real saints in the church would bring glory to the Lord, and at the same time, bring immense joy to his heart. They would become his crown of rejoicing, something he would gladly lay down at the feet of Jesus. It is on this wonderful event that Paul could hang his hope. Because, in the words of Mrs Anne Ross Cousin:

The bride eyes not her garment,
But her dear bridegroom's face;
I will not gaze at glory
But on my King of grace;
Not at the crown he giveth,
But on his pierced hand:
The Lamb is all the glory
Of Immanuel's land.

A church where love is manifested

Paul gives us some assurances about affliction that are neither bland nor blasé, but biblical; and in the second half of the chapter, where he focuses on truth about the tempter, we shall discover some fascinating insights into our age-old enemy, our adversary, the devil.

Basically, it is all about finding our feet and learning to stand on them. We need to be grounded in the faith, so that when the turbulent winds of trial blow in our face, we do not fall flat. Consequently, Paul shows us the path to spiritual maturity, the road down which we must go to attain spiritual advancement. Charles Thomas Studd (1860-1931), famous England cricketer and one of the Cambridge Seven, was on the same wavelength when he recognised that ' … mere soul-saving is easy; what is difficult is making those converts into soldiers, saints, and soul winners!'

The key word is located in verses 2 and 13, *establish*. The key verse is verse 8, *For now we live, if you are standing fast in the Lord*. There is one phrase which appears five times in the space of ten verses – *your faith* – that is both significant and suggestive:

- the profession of your faith (verse 2)
- the examination of your faith (verse 5)
- the proclamation of your faith (verse 6)
- the consolation of your faith (verse 7)
- the additions to your faith (verse 10)

3:1

Absence makes the heart

It is patently obvious that Paul's heart pined for them. He knew a measure of felt pain because he could not be with them, he was distraught. In fact, it became so bad that he was buckling under, it seemed as though he could not stand the strain one minute more. The sound of silence was far from golden, it was unbearable and the suspense of wondering how things were going was proving too much for him to handle. The whole experience was pushing him over the edge.

Paul was much more than cheesed off. He was so frustrated that he found himself at breaking point. About to snap, he longed for a measure of release and relief. He could not pick up the mobile phone and call them for a chinwag, nor could he jump on his Harley and ride north. Poor

Paul, he could not even communicate by email, Skype, or WhatsApp! Imagine life before the Internet and Messenger!

At this point the preacher was in Athens, one of the world's oldest cities, and on the verge of going further south to Corinth, but his heart was up north in Thessalonica. He knew where he preferred to be, where he wanted to be, because they meant so much to him. That explains why he feels totally overwhelmed with an abject sense of inconsolable desolation. Abandoned. Deflated. Alone. And one of the worst things about loneliness is that you cannot run away from it.

The thought behind the Greek word for *left* is that it describes what happens when parents die and their children are left orphans. The implication behind this refreshingly honest comment is that Paul is passing through something akin to bereavement. In other words, a big part of him is missing. That spells sacrifice!

In 1858 Scottish missionary John G Paton and his wife sailed for the New Hebrides Islands in the South Pacific (now called Vanuatu). Against the advice of many who saw this endeavour as a suicide mission, Paton and his wife left their families, their friends, and the comforts of home for a strange and distant land. Their consuming passion was to share the gospel of Jesus Christ with the native peoples, among whom were thousands of barbaric cannibals. Three months after arriving in the islands, his wife died. One week later his infant son also died. Paton eventually remarried and after a short time away, returned to the Islands with his new bride. Together, they spent the next 41 years faithfully sharing the love of Jesus. Today more than eighty percent of the inhabitants of Vanuatu identify themselves as Christian in large part due to the sacrifices of Paton.

An incident early in his life gives us some insight into the convictions of this man. Before leaving for the New Hebrides, Paton was warned by one of his fellow Scotsmen that the cannibals would almost certainly eat him. His reply is classic: 'Mr Dickson, you are advanced in years now, and your own prospect is soon to be laid in the grave, there to be eaten by worms. I confess to you, that if I can but live and die serving and honouring the Lord Jesus, it will make no difference to me whether I am eaten by cannibals or by worms; and in the Great Day my resurrection body will arise as fair as yours in the likeness of our risen Redeemer.'

John G Paton and Paul were both made from the same mould. Paul's willingness to sacrifice for the sake of the church is seen in his attitude here in verses 1-3. A glimpse of the same outlook is unearthed in 2 Corinthians 11:23-28. For him, personal comforts were secondary to those of the church. His thinking is gospel-centred because he focused on others! This is self-denying, sacrificial love in one of its finest exhibits. Gilbert Keith Chesterton (1874-1936) once remarked, 'How much larger your life would be if your self could become smaller in it.' As James H Grant notes, 'This is precisely what was motivating Paul, and it is a powerful testimony to the gospel. It should stir us to deny ourselves.' So what does he do?

3:2

All alone in Athens

Well, rather than go himself – the easy option – Paul stays where he is, and instead, sends young Timothy on his behalf. He was willing to adjust his plans to accomplish God's plans. That is what believers do! Not an easy decision for a man in his sandals to make, but his track record is exemplary. On past experience, Athens was not Paul's favourite location, he had been alone there once before. On that occasion, his escort left him to find his own way about town: a painful, unnerving experience it proved to be (Acts 17:15).

Such a city was a demanding place for any evangelist as it was a hotbed of intellectual activity, and his whole being felt oppressed and provoked by the unbelievable idolatry that prevailed in the place. It was home to more than 30,000 different gods. It was also a cesspool of iniquity and a philosopher's playground. This was a university town, with more than its fair share of critics. It was home to Plato's Academy and Aristotle's Lyceum, perhaps the birthplace of democracy.

That said, his sermon on Mars Hill, at a meeting of the Areopagus, is quite brilliant. Preacher Paul took them on, using their own intellectual games, and beat them hollow (Acts 17:22-34). He started where they were, the unknown God, but he quickly took them right to the heart of the Christian gospel by telling them that God in Jesus Christ can be known. Paul had a handful of converts in Athens but it was not overly encouraging; no wonder there is no epistle to the Athenians!

Pastor Paul did not have any realistic alternative, he was suffering from information underload; so, bearing in mind his insatiable thirst for news, this was the best plan he could come up with. Even though he shrank from it, it was the lesser of two evils. He knew that Timothy would be able to see them, and when he got there, he could enquire as to their spiritual health.

Paul is not unduly concerned about their comfort, he is not too alarmed about their welfare, he is not stressed out about their prosperity. Those things are important, but not all-important. It is their faith that he is interested in; it is their daily relationship with the Lord that matters most to him. Surely that is symptomatic of a father's love for his spiritual children.

Short-term missionary

He could not have chosen anyone better than Timothy. As they say, he was a chip off the old block, a man after his own heart. Actually, what old man Paul has to say about the much younger Timothy in Philippians 2:20 speaks volumes, 'I have no one like him, who will be genuinely concerned for your welfare.' He was Paul's troubleshooter, an emissary, a kind of special agent. Paul reckoned if something was broken in their local fellowship, this young man was the ideal person to fix it.

It is intriguing to see how Paul describes someone a number of years his junior. After all, he was old enough to be his father, and more often than not, he treated him in a fatherly way! This microchip description stores a world of priceless information about Timothy's character. Paul gives him a superb reference.

- *Our brother*

He was a saved man in the family of God. It is obvious they enjoyed a sweet relationship with each other. It was a sheer joy and genuine delight for Paul to have him as his right-hand man. We see something here of the dignity of his role in life for he is the Lord's. In spite of his youthful years, Timothy had a stable relationship with the Lord.

- *God's co-worker*

He was a team player, they were fellows! He was a servant, unafraid of hard work. This man had the sterling qualities needed to effectively minister to young believers. He had patience, and lots of it, for Timothy realised you get the chicken by hatching the egg, not by smashing it. His first-rate dedication to whatever assignment the Lord entrusted to him was combined with a measure of love and grace in his heart. Timothy would later become Paul's protégé and one of the early church's finest pastors.

What was his task? One, it was to strengthen the believers as they were weak at the knees. The Greek verb translated as *to establish* was a technical term for the consolidation and building up of new converts; it means 'to shore up, to buttress'. These good folk needed built up. Two, he was also to *exhort* the church because they were low in spirit. They needed a boost and he was despatched in order to comfort them and cheer them up.

3:3-4

The rough with the smooth

The primary objective of Timothy's mission was so *that no one be moved by these afflictions*. Paul yearns for them to stand firm and stand fast in the Lord. He has a fair idea what they are passing through and he is all too aware of the devastating consequences such difficult times can bring in their wake. He knows at best it could make them; or at worst, it could break them.

The Greek word translated as *moved* was used at first of dogs wagging their tail and so came to mean 'flatter, or fawn upon' and therefore 'deceive'. Satan is more dangerous when he flatters than when he frowns. Paul was extremely worried that their sufferings might lead them astray from Christ. John Stott suggests, 'Perhaps the best way to protect people from being upset by tribulation is to remind them that it is a necessary part of our Christian vocation.'

Nagging away at the back of Paul's mind was the ugly thought that they might have succumbed to this unrelenting pressure. Would they be shaken to the core by their experiences? Would they be persuaded to abandon their Christian profession? If they did, life in the short term would be a whole lot easier for them! Perhaps, like the followers of

Jesus in every period of history, they were tempted to jump to unwarranted conclusions about the character and nature of the Lord himself: either he does not have the power or the will to prevent the suffering, or he is not strong enough to shield me from tribulation, or he does not care what happens to me anyway! Paul's unqualified response is that suffering is an integral part, an essential component, of the unfolding purpose of God for all his children. It goes with the territory. As Thomas Watson notes, 'The holiness of the saints will not excuse them from suffering.'

It's hurting, Lord

Paul moves on to deal with the perplexing problem of affliction. *For you yourselves know that we are destined for this. For when we were with you, we kept telling you beforehand that we were to suffer affliction, just as it has come to pass, and just as you know.*

The apostle handles trouble with a mix of sensitivity and common sense. He is both tactful and tender. He gives them a word of assurance by informing them that affliction and trial is inevitable for the Christian. There is no getting away from it. The Christian life is not a Sunday school picnic nor is it one big spiritual Disneyland. It was never intended to be. Following Jesus is not an easy alternative to life. The chances of us being 'carried to the skies on flowery beds of ease' are nil (1 Peter 4:12-13). Rather, says Paul, troubles and trials will come, and when they do, they will hurt. We cannot avoid them or play hide and seek with them. They are part and parcel of every believer's experience (John 15:18-20).

They are our portion, according to Philippians 1:29, where Paul says, 'For it has been granted to you that for the sake of Christ you should not only believe in him but also suffer for his sake.' In a different sense, they are a privilege, according to Philippians 3:10, where Paul describes them as 'the fellowship of sharing in Christ's sufferings' (NIV). And in a strange kind of way, they are our power, as in 2 Corinthians 12:9, where Paul confirms that '[God's] grace is sufficient for you, for [his] power is made perfect in weakness. Therefore I will boast all the more gladly of my weaknesses, so that the power of Christ may rest upon me.' In that light, pain is not our enemy, it is our friend. We should respond to trial and hardship like the sage who lived on a tiny island in the Pacific. When asked by the residents how they should prepare for a rapidly approaching tidal wave, he replied, 'We would all do well to learn how to live underwater.' In such hair-raising moments, we hold one another up, and we pick one another up.

Divine intruder

Paul talks about our attitude, our mindset, by saying that we were *destined* for such times of disquiet. If you like, we had them coming to us, they were coming our way, come what may. It is not the luck of the draw, nor is it a question of pulling the shortest straw. These traumatic experiences were not just sheer bad luck or even an uncontrollable conspiracy.

When trials intrude into your life and mine and invade our privacy, they are not accidents waiting to happen.

Rather, they are sent to us by divine appointment. C H Spurgeon observed that 'God's love letters are often sent in black-trimmed envelopes.' He also acknowledged that 'God sometimes puts his children to bed in the dark.'

I love eating rhubarb, especially when it is freshly pulled from the garden plot! Do you know how they produce it commercially? In order to ensure a good harvest of rhubarb for the market, they plunge the plants into darkness and so the stalks shoot up as they quest for light. 'Sometimes,' according to David Strain, 'when God wants to make us fruitful servants, he brings us into a season of darkness and suffering and trial and conflict and pain.'

Nothing happens to us by chance, and there is nothing that can be slotted into a pigeonhole labelled 'coincidence'. Everything – the best of times, the worst of times – what we like, what we do not like – is a vital part of the outworking of God's plan for our lives. If anything, they are a God-incidence. They are well within the scope of the perfect will of God and can all be attributed to the sovereign providence of a loving heavenly Father.

My Father planned it all

When we find ourselves with more questions than answers in our mind, we need to recognise God's purpose in it all. In God's goodness he has something to teach us, there is always a timely lesson to be learned. Remember Joseph? His brothers meant it for evil, but the Lord had a few other ideas up his sleeve (Genesis 50:20). From the divine vantage point, it would ultimately be for Joseph's good and benefit.

And it was! It is Romans 8:28 being activated as a powerful principle in our lives. Behind the dark threatening clouds, the sun still shines brightly.

We also need to realise his perfection. David was thoroughly convinced of this. After he was hunted and hounded by his enemies, he was able to write, 'This God – his way is perfect' (Psalm 18:30). Left to himself, it is not the path David would have chosen, but it is the one that God mapped out for him. And with the benefit of hindsight – 20/20 vision – his testimony is unerringly accurate. Thomas Watson makes the point that 'afflictions promote holiness. The more the diamond is cut, the more it sparkles.'

And we need to rest on the divine promise. When we compare Romans 8:18 with all that we are going through at this point in time, everything is brought sharply into focus. Paul says, 'I consider that the sufferings of this present time are not worth comparing with the glory that is to be revealed to us.' The problems remain, but they last only for a brief moment in light of an eternity spent in the near presence of the Lord. It may be devastating and demeaning down here, but it cannot be compared to the glory that will be ours when we reach the other side. The hurts of this life will be followed by hallelujahs in the next!

Bespoke trials

When we do all of that, we can rejoice in God's gracious provision. The Lord knows how much we can take, and he will send us no more than we can bear. Our trials are tailor-made, personalised, for God in his infinite wisdom deals with us individually. Frederick Brotherton Meyer (1847-1929) expressed this truth sweetly and succinctly, 'The sweetest scents are only obtained by tremendous pressure, the fairest flowers grow amid Alpine snow-solitudes, the rarest gems have suffered longest from the lapidary's wheel, the noblest statues have borne most blows of the chisel.' The lesson is: the Lord does not make the back for the burden, he makes each burden to suit the back. The good news is, according to the 'prince of expositors' Alexander MacLaren, 'If God sends us on stony paths, he will provide us with strong shoes.'

'Til the storm passes by

Paul makes an assessment of the situation. The Greek word used for *affliction* speaks of intense pain, it conveys the idea of crippling heartache and enduring hardness. It has the basic thought of being often found in a perilous situation where the pressures come from without and within. It is when we feel buffeted from every possible direction. It does not matter where we turn, we cannot run away from it. When troubles come, our comfort zone gets the squeeze. We know all about it when it happens.

God is not in the least bit interested in watching our faith get torpedoed by all sorts of trials; the fact is, every test is designed by God to elasticise our faith. When real faith is stretched, it does not break; and when it is pressed, it does not fail. As Paul himself admitted, we may be knocked down, but we will never be knocked out. Not for us the shame of being counted out on the canvas (2 Corinthians 4:9). 'Praise

God for the hammer, the file and the furnace,' concludes Samuel Rutherford. Perhaps the moving words written from the heart of Andraè Crouch (1942-2015) sum it up best:

I thank God for the mountains
And I thank him for the valleys,
I thank him for the storms he brought me through.
For if I'd never had a problem,
I wouldn't know that he could solve them,
I'd never know what faith in God could do.

He continues:

Through it all, through it all,
O I've learned to trust in Jesus,
I've learned to trust in God.
Through it all, through it all,
I've learned to depend upon his word.

3:5

Truth about the tempter

Paul then reminds them of his prime reason for sending Timothy on a special fact-finding mission. *For this reason, when I could bear it no longer, I sent to learn about your faith.* In other words, it was all becoming too much for Paul: he had had enough, he could not stand the heat any longer so it was best for him to get out of the kitchen! In moments like that, we think we have to justify our feelings and Paul in this instance was no exception. He is a man like the rest of us!

Paul changes tack and bares his heart as he opens up and shares with us the major concern that gripped him, he is afraid *that somehow the tempter had tempted you and our labour would be in vain.* The Greek word translated *tempted* can be neutral in the sense of 'test' or negative in the sense of 'lure'. God tests, Satan lures! Because it is obvious that Paul is talking about the devil, the avowed intent of the enemy is to disable their faith by deceitfully drawing them into sin; he wants to disarm them by testing them with a host of malicious intentions.

Paul did not at any time underestimate the power of Satan. He knew only too well that what had earlier occurred in the idyllic setting of Eden could also repeat itself in their little church fellowship. Paul reminds us with some straight-talking that the devil is alive and kicking. If we have any lingering doubts, we need only ask the good folk in the church at Thessalonica for their considered opinion. They are in a position to respond because they are the ones who have been on the receiving end. Day after day the devil made a nuisance of himself in their extremely delicate situation. No matter where they turned, no matter what they did, he never seemed too far away. He was ever loitering with intent. A real pain in their neck, a thorn in their flesh. His overt aim was always to make them stumble. The devil was only happy when they were the epitome of misery. The devil was committed to wiping the smile off their faces.

Ring-fencing the devil

God's policy is unmistakably clear and concise with regard to the tempter:

- His scope is God-determined – he can go so far and no further.
- His sphere is God-defined – he can go so near and no closer.
- His strength is God-dictated – he can do so much and no more.

Each of these insuperable truths is vitally important to our understanding of the work of Satan in relation to the Christian. Having said that, we rejoice at this point in time that, because of Calvary, the tempter's power is broken.

Ever wondered, what is the devil's line of attack? How does he strike at us? Paul said elsewhere in 2 Corinthians 2:9-11, 'This is why I wrote ... so that we would not be outwitted by Satan; for we are not ignorant of his designs.'

On the Wilde side

The story is told of the boy whose mother told him not to go swimming as he had a bad head cold. The doorbell rang and Johnny went off with his friends. Later on his mother passed the spot where the boys were splashing around in the pond. She could not believe her eyes when she saw her son in the water alongside them. She stopped the car and shouted for him to come and explain himself.

Dripping wet, he blurted out to his mother, 'Mum, I'm sorry, I didn't mean to disobey you.' She retorted, 'Well, if you didn't mean to disobey me, why did you bring your swimming trunks with you? Why didn't you leave them at home in the bottom drawer?' Johnny thought for a moment and then he said, 'I'm really sorry, mum, but I brought them with me just in case I was tempted!'

It goes without saying but temptation is the oldest of all the internal conflicts that rage in the heart of man. Sometimes, like Johnny, it seems we tempt ourselves, or at least we put ourselves in harm's way. Doug Barnett challenges us, 'If you don't want the devil to tempt you with forbidden fruit, you had better keep out of his orchard.' It does not matter who we are, it stalks every single one of us. None of us is immune! I am as vulnerable as the man next door.

It was the humorist Oscar Wilde (1854-1900) who quipped, 'I can resist everything except temptation.' He was not the only one who had to cope with that particular weakness, as the same was true of Mark Antony (83-30 BC). He was known as the silver-throated orator of Rome. He was credited with the accolade of being a brilliant man, as well as being a strong leader and courageous soldier. Having said that, he had one gaping hole in his personality for he lacked strength of character. On the outside, he was powerful and impressive; on the inside, weak and vulnerable. His tutor is reputed to have been so enraged on one occasion that he shouted at him, 'O Marcus, O colossal child, able to conquer the world but unable to resist a temptation.'

Most of us know the sequel to the story, for his most widely known and costly temptation sailed up the river to him on a barge. Cleopatra captured his unguarded heart and their sinful relationship cost him his wife, his place as a world leader and, ultimately, his life.

Surprise, surprise

Now, when it comes to our door, the enemy may choose to surprise us. The classic example is David and Bathsheba. It was the most unlikely moment when David was caught napping. His guard was down. He was torn apart in a moment of time when least expecting it. It only took a split second for him to court spiritual disaster. In such moments, we need to follow Joseph's example and do a runner! Pastor Al Martin's assessment is helpful when he tells us 'there is a time for holy running.'

The devil may use the siege method. His intentions are crystal clear from Daniel 7:25 where we are reminded that 'he shall wear out the saints.' Constant pressure can crack us. We break up, then break down, and he breaks in. He tells us that our circumstances are far too difficult, and our past failures have weakened us too much. He highlights our inability to overcome some besetting sin. His tactics are to wear us down until we can take no more. The devil is no fool, he knows our weakest point and he can always locate with pinpoint accuracy the chink in our armour. Satan knows our Achilles heel.

Another tactic is for him to use the subtle line of attack. The wily devil is the past master of disguise. When he approaches us, dressed as an angel of light, he makes sin look innocuously innocent. Remember our first parents, Adam and Eve, in the pacific Garden of Eden? Instead of fresh fruit, they found toxic poison; instead of a contented smile of satisfaction, they found hang-your-head shame; instead of immense pleasure, they found intense pain.

In Matthew 4 he attempted to trip up the Lord Jesus by adopting similar scare tactics. He told him to turn the stones into bread and go *before* the will of God; he told him to throw himself down from the pinnacle of the temple and go *beyond* the will of God; he told him to bow down before him and see the kingdoms of the world and go *behind* the will of God. We know the sequel! Thank God, the adversary was unsuccessful on all three counts. Some words penned by Edward Albert Barnes (1842-93) help focus our thinking:

Trust God when the tempter is near,
Trust in him for grace to turn aside,
Trust God mid the billows of life,
A refuge to provide.

Now we see why Paul did what he did by despatching young Timothy as his special envoy. Like pieces in a jigsaw, it fits neatly into place. It all comes together, and when it does, it makes a lot of sense.

3:6

Just what the doctor ordered

At this juncture Timothy has returned, his important

assignment ably carried out. *But now that Timothy has come to us from you, and has brought us the good news of your faith and love and reported that you always remember us kindly and long to see us, as we long to see you.*

I love what John Calvin (1509-64) said about those two words, *faith* and *love*. 'In them,' he noted, 'the apostle gives a brief summary of all godliness.' Evangelist Tom Hayes notes that faith and love run side by side in Timothy's report:

- They go together (verse 6).
- They grow together (verse 8).
- They flow together (verse 9).

Timothy has done the job Paul asked him to do and the news he brings could not be better. The phrase *good news* is the same we use when we speak of the glorious gospel of Christ. Glad tidings. This is the only time the word is used in the New Testament when it does not specifically refer to the gospel. When Paul heard Timothy's glowing report, he felt as if he was being saved all over again. Such is the Damascus Road effect it had on him.

Without hyperbole, or any stretching of the imagination, or any hint of exaggeration, Paul is like a brand-new man. Euphorically ecstatic, deliriously jubilant, and totally rejuvenated. This was the morale booster he desperately needed. It was just what the doctor ordered, a proverbial tonic to his soul, it really thrilled him. It was comparable to him being drenched with a refreshing spring shower.

Hearts of gold, feet of clay

We are inclined to forget that Paul was made of the same material as the rest of us. We elevate these men into supersaints, when the fact of the matter is they are made of exactly the same stuff as we lesser lights. We put the Lord's servants on a pedestal when in reality their feet are standing on the same old world as ours.

When we read between the lines, it would appear that Paul was having one of his off-days; he was on a real downer. The blues! He was utterly depressed and extremely disheartened. Discouraged to the nth degree. His outlook changed, however, when he heard the brilliant news from Timothy. It did the trick. His battery recharged, it set the adrenalin flowing through his veins. Now he is back to his usual good self. To Paul, dumped right in the middle of his arid wasteland of personal loneliness, Timothy's report was a lush oasis of hope. What an encouragement! The preacher man got a second wind.

Like cold water to a thirsty soul

Timothy has talked about their *faith and love* and given a clear indication that they were really going on well with the Lord. They were enthusiastically reaching out to others in the community. In many areas of gospel ministry, they were like the pioneer of modern missions, William Carey (1761-1834), in that they lengthened the cords and strengthened the stakes. They were tirelessly active in gospel work. People on the go, running and gunning for God.

On a spiritual level they were alive and well, standing firm against the world's erosion. They had pleasant memories of Paul and his brief visit with them. It meant so much to Paul because at this point he was feeling low and rejected, dejected and forgotten. He had his moments when he wondered, is it really worth it? There were many times in his life when he felt as though he was well past his sell-by date. His mind was in overdrive on the fast lane of life where so many issues were blown out of all proportion. Mind you, the longer he wallowed in his deep slimy pit of despair, the more introverted he became. He felt as if he had really blown it big time and that he was just a wretched failure coming apart at the seams.

Timothy reassures him that the folk remember him with fond affection, and they, likewise, hoped that their paths would cross again. They wanted to be with him as much as he wanted to be with them. Whether we are a Paul or not, we all need to feel accepted and sense that our ministry is appreciated. The best of men are only men at best! The question is: What impact did this all have on the apostle? I think it was like a bridge, in that it helped him reach the other side.

3:7-8

Iron sharpens iron

Paul is enormously encouraged for he writes, *For this reason, brothers, in all our distress and affliction we have been comforted about you through your faith.* He talks openly about his personal distress. The idea wrapped up in that Greek word is the kind of trouble that has a crushing effect on a man; he felt as though he had been submerged to such an extent that all talk of keeping his head above water was nonsense. The way he felt, even snorkelling was nigh impossible.

He then speaks of his persecution, which means the kind of mitigating pressure that has a choking effect on us; he felt strangled. Suppressed. Both words are used together in Job 15:24 where they speak of one who is so terrified and overpowered that their hair stands on end. We find that paralysing combination in the LXX (shorthand for the Septuagint, the Greek translation of the Old Testament).

He was left breathless, as it were. He felt stifled. Muffled. Suffocated. His blood ran cold. But this was the best news he could have possibly heard. Why did Paul feel the way he did? As I hinted earlier, he is in Athens, which is not the most user-friendly place to be if you happen to be a preacher, and to make matters a million times worse, the poor guy is very much on his own. Paul has had one harrowing experience after another of apparent defeat since he set foot on the soil of the continent of Europe. His situation seemed to spiral from bad to worse.

Sure, he promptly responded to the Macedonian call, but he got a lot more than he bargained for: it was one dreadful trial hard on the heels of another. Any clear-thinking man would automatically question all this in his own mind. He could be forgiven for asking himself:

- Did I get it wrong?
- Did I misread the leading of God?

- Did I mistake what God was saying to me?

So this fantastic news from Timothy was just the pick-me-up he needed. His life was wrapped up in theirs to such a degree that he was one with them. That is the gist of his comments in verse 8 where he seemingly shouts at the top of his voice, *For now we live, if you are standing fast in the Lord.*

No matter what standpoint we view it from, this is body ministry, pure and simple. Paul is energised to such a degree that it would appear he has been given a new lease of life, as a heavy burden has been lifted off his sagging shoulders. That phrase speaks volumes for it tells us that a troubled, tension-filled servant of Christ felt able to relax one more time, to breathe normally. Perhaps he also felt that, after all, his life was not in vain, that in laying it out for the sake of the gospel he was not spending himself to no purpose.

3:9-10

Lost for words

Because of this welcome development, he is able to break forth into a paean of praise. Paul asks a rhetorical question: *For what thanksgiving can we return to God for you, for all the joy that we feel for your sake before our God, as we pray most earnestly night and day that we may see you face to face and supply what is lacking in your faith.* He says a sincere thank you to the Lord for them, and it is worth noting that this is his first reaction to the uplifting news that Timothy has shared with him. It naturally leads him into praise-and-thanksgiving mode. It not only seemed the proper thing to do, it was the right thing to do! This gospel community mean more to him than words can tell.

He is not speechless, but he is lost for words when he thinks about them. He says, *for what thanksgiving can we return to God for you?* It would have been so easy for Paul to have taken a different line. He could, for instance, have congratulated the young believers in their staying power. He could have patted himself on the back and waxed lyrical in personal congratulation, 'See what a great gospel church I've planted!' In fact, the approach adopted in this passage was typical of Paul, for it illustrates that he understood the reality of the situation as it was. God made these believers what they were. The credit was his and his alone. The Lord enabled them to step up to the plate.

As a direct result, Paul pours out a never-ending stream of prayer, adoration, and thanksgiving as an offering to God, knowing that he will never be able to fully repay the obligation. God has blessed him more than tongue can tell, and the folk in Thessalonica bear eloquent testimony to that. The Psalmist in Psalm 116:12 expressed the same idea when he posed the leading question: 'How can I repay the Lord for all his goodness to me?'

Furthermore, there is wisdom and pastoral sense in Paul's accentuating the positive kind of approach. To be assured that a mature believer like Paul sincerely thanks God for us is a tremendous crank up to most of us. Simply wonderful. It introduces the feel-good factor back into our lives, but there again, that is the genius of grace. It is mightily encouraging to us, without pandering to our innate tendency to self-promotion. In passing, I believe that Paul was immensely gladdened by the spiritual quality of his friends. As someone has said, 'Christian excellence is a great help to others for it reminds them that the power of God is at work in a human life. Thus it is not only a source of encouragement but a spur and a challenge.'

Four habits of a successful pray-er

The Scottish Presbyterian preacher Thomas Chalmers (1780-1847) noted that 'prayer does not just enable us to do a greater work for God. Prayer is a greater work for God.' Paul prayed earnestly for them. He did not get down at the side of his bed every night and say, 'Lord, bless my friends up there in Thessalonica, period.' Many people pray like the man who said, 'Lord, bless me and my wife, our son John and his wife, us four and no more!' On bended knees, Paul considered seriously what they were going through. He set the problem before the throne of grace and reminded the Lord of his many promises. Paul took time to reflect on their many needs, both corporate and individual.

Paul prayed frequently for them. We read it was *night and day*. That means while he was working on his goat-hair tents, and while he was walking the dusty, pot-holed streets of the city, his prayers for them flowed freely out of a heart of concern and love.

Paul prayed specifically for them. He was definite in his prayer requests. He knew what he wanted for them: he wants to see them again. That is the deep longing of his heart, as there was a refreshing spontaneity about their relationship. They always brought a smile to his face, never a frown. They were number one on his priority list.

A sense of belonging

It shows how much the church meant to him. That is the dynamic relationship we should all be pursuing in our regular place of worship. When we meet one another, it is wonderful to say, 'Thank you, Lord, he's my brother, she's my sister.' It is not a backslapping service, nor is it a mutual admiration society. It is a simple realisation that since we belong to the Lord, we really do belong to one another. Maybe we should take a few moments even now and pray, 'Bind us together, Lord, bind us together with cords that cannot be broken.'

At the end of the day and at the end of his prayer, his all-consuming passion for them is that they might grow in grace and go on well with the Lord. He wants them to make spiritual headway, and that by leaps and bounds. To progress. To develop. Backpedalling puts us in reverse. And there is no mileage gained by standing still. Forward is to be their watchword.

Faith in working clothes

Faith is like a muscle, we either use it or lose it! It is equally true to say that the more we use faith, the stronger it becomes. Faith must be exercised or it will atrophy. Perhaps the best example of that principle is enshrined in the life of the patriarch Abraham:

- He believed God when he had no idea where he was going to end up (Hebrews 11:8).

- He believed God when he did not have a clue how it would all pan out (Hebrews 11:11).

- He believed God when he could not work out why God led him the way that he did (Hebrews 11:17-19).

God will test our faith to exercise it; not to destroy it, but to develop it. A faith that cannot be tested is a faith that cannot be trusted. The two are like a hand in a glove. God uses the difficulties we face to refine us and make us more like Jesus. Whatever we are called to go through, we need to remember that God keeps his eye on the clock and the temperature gauge; he knows how long and how hot is just about right for us in the steamy sauna of life.

Missing link

The glaring problem they faced was that there was something missing or *lacking* in their faith. The Greek word for *supply* is rich in meaning and varied in usage. It means 'to fit together, to join, to restore, to repair, to equip'. For example, it is used of reconciling political differences, it is a surgical term for setting bones, it describes the repairing of fishing nets, and it is used when making military and naval preparations.

It would appear as though Paul is acting as a medical doctor applying healing balm to people's souls; or he could be seen as a fisherman mending the broken twine of belief; perhaps he could even be portrayed as a military commander instructing the believers to do battle with Satan. That was what Paul prayed, that they might be able to supply what was lacking in their faith.

Imagine his undiluted joy when a relatively short time later he writes them a second letter and he is able to say that God answered his prayer. 'We ought always to give thanks to God for you, brothers, as is right, because your faith is growing abundantly' (2 Thessalonians 1:3). Let me give you some characteristics of true faith, it is:

- Restful – the soul can be satisfied in its secure relationship with Christ (Hebrews 4:3).

- Joyful – we are glad that Jesus is our Lord and Saviour (1 Peter 1:8).

- Hopeful – our faith teaches us that, whilst we are blessed at present, the best is yet to come (Hebrews 11:1).

- Loving – Christian qualities complement and encourage each other (Galatians 5:6).

- Practical – even though it is inward, it will always show itself in an outward fashion (James 2:20).

- Patient – faith affirms that God is the perfect time-keeper for he is never early or late, he is always on schedule (Hebrews 11:6).

- Victorious – we are walking in the train of his triumph (1 John 5:4).

- Vocal – when we speak, our faith is immediately strengthened (2 Corinthians 4:13).

- Ever-growing – the more we exercise it the stronger it will become (2 Corinthians 10:15).

Faith is not a leap in the dark; it is not a gushy feeling we have at the end of a good meeting. Faith is something that rests on the solid promises of God, then acts on them. Acts of obedience to the word of God are acts of faith. Do we want more faith? Well, there are no shortcuts, read and then obey the word of God, and the more we do that, we can watch our faith grow!

3:11

Can God? God can!

Here is a moving reminder that Paul has come to the end of himself. He has an overwhelming feeling of personal inadequacy and inability. He knows that even though he cannot do it, God can. Is anything too hard for the Lord? He tossed the ball back into God's court, for he is the master of the situation; he is able to solve the crisis and undo the tangled mess. It is a well-thought-out decision on Paul's part to say, 'Lord, it's over to you!' That is reflected in his sincere desire, *Now may our God and Father himself, and our Lord Jesus, direct our way to you.*

He knew in his heart of hearts that only God could open up the way ahead. Such consolation. The path was littered with many obstacles and lined with many immovable hindrances. On a human level, it was impossible. However, it is in these no-go and no-win areas that God delights to prove his stunning ability; he specialises in dealing with situations just like these. He can get us where he wants us to be. Only God himself could make the impossible possible. As Mark Howell reminds us, 'We must trust God to do what is in his best interest and not ours. We are not architects for *our* kingdom; we are ambassadors for *his* kingdom.'

What about his challenge? Well, Paul is resigned to the will of God. Kicking in doors that God is unwilling to open will only lead to disaster. Ask Moses what it cost him to kick in a door at Meribah (Numbers 20:2-13). He believes that God's way is always the best way. For him there is no viable alternative, anything else is unthinkable. It may not be the easiest trail to walk down, but for Paul, God's way is always the preferred option. There is no Plan B. He reckons it is much better to be alone with God than to be in the crowd without him.

God is bigger than all our problems. Before a transcendent God, they are like measly grasshoppers. There is no hill too high and no valley too low for him. He is the God who causes Jericho's walls to tumble, and when he does not bring them crashing down, he jumps over them (Psalm 18:29). He is, therefore, God of the impregnable and God of the impassable! He is God of all our tears and fears.

3:12

Love, love, love

Operation Agape is launched in this verse. Paul's desire for them is that their love may abound. This is getting our hands dirty in the service of Jesus. It is getting our feet wet in ministering to others in his name. In this context, we need to remember that our response to suffering is never far from his mind. Sometimes our times of suffering can turn into times of selfishness. We can so quickly become insular, parochial, and self-centred. We become so demanding on those around us that we are hard to live with.

You see, what life does to us depends on what life finds in us. Nothing reveals the true heart of man like the furnace of affliction. Trials will bring out the best in us; they can also bring out the worst. It depends how we react and respond.

When the going gets tough, the tough get going! But where? Some people build a 20-foot wall that cannot be scaled. They shut themselves in and cut themselves off from others. Others build a bridge, enabling them to reach out to others. When they do that, they are brought closer to the Lord and to his people. To quote Westy Egmont, 'Conflict plus love equals growth.'

Paul prayed, *may the Lord make you increase and abound in love for one another and for all*. And, wonder of wonders, his prayer was answered. We read all about it in 2 Thessalonians 1:3 where the apostle writes, '… the love of every one of you for one another is increasing.'

Yes, it was Paul's request that their love might be full and overflowing: a love for one another, a love for those outside the family of God, a love for the unloved and unlovable; for none of us should feel as though people do not care. Jew and Greek, Christian and non-believer. The world is not waiting for advice on how to solve its problems. It is waiting for someone to listen to it and love it. It does not matter who or what they are or where they are from, we can love them through Jesus. Actually, it is a command to be obeyed. This was the badge worn on the lapel of their lives. They wore their religion on their sleeves. The mark of a healthy gospel church is when others are able to say, 'See how they love each other, and all people' (John 13:34-35).

Out on a limb

Abounding love must never be bound. It is always reaching out. It expands and is expansive. It is all-embracing. Love always looks after number two, not exclusively after number one. It goes past the call and claim of duty. It goes far beyond the suggested second or third mile. When we share love and show love to other people in an unconditional, unselfish manner, we always walk away the winner. Not only are others enriched, so are we. Duty makes us do things well, but love takes us to a new level when it makes us do them beautifully.

Be realistic! Nine times out of ten when we love this way, we become vulnerable. And exposed. And sometimes wounded. But if we never step out on a limb with people and take a risk, we shall never grasp the yummy fruit of nourishing relationships. In the final analysis, it is God touching the lives of men and women, boys and girls, through ordinary people like us. I appreciate the way Charles Swindoll puts it as he uses each of the letters in an acrostic fashion:

- **L** is for us to listen. That shows itself when we respect and accept people enough to graciously hear what they have to say.

- **O** is for overlook. This says we should be quick to pass over and forgive the minor, unpleasant flaws in other people's lives.

- **V** is for value, which indicates a respect and honour we have for the other person. We appreciate them for who they are, and we see in them someone for whom the Saviour has died.

- **E** reminds us to express love, for it is demonstrative. We do not just feel love or say loving things; we show it by doing what is best for the other person.

The gospel church in Thessalonica was: a place where faith was vibrant, a fellowship pulsating with life, a congregation where love was warmly felt.

3:13

The morning after

Paul's final petition is that their lives might be holy. Again, this request is closely linked to the fast-approaching return of our Lord. It is the second advent of Jesus Christ that is brought sharply into focus, putting everything into proper perspective. He longs that when they stand before the Lord they will be *blameless in holiness*. When someone is blameless, there are no blemishes on their life. When someone is holy, there are no blots on their character. Holiness is his lifestyle.

Paul looks forward to that day when we shall be called to give an account of the service we have rendered to the Lord (2 Corinthians 5:10). This is a personal interview with Jesus. Paul reminds them that they are responsible down here, for they will be held accountable up there. He wants to present us as 'a pure virgin' to Christ (2 Corinthians 11:2). He wants his bride to be a glorious church, 'a radiant church ... without stain or wrinkle or any other blemish' (Ephesians 5:27). Stains are caused by defilement on the outside, blemishes are caused by decay on the inside.

American pastor, Kevin DeYoung, acknowledges that 'God's children will never be as pristinely and unfailingly holy as God, but we should be holy. Christians should display a consistent pattern of obedience, along with a quick habit of going to God for cleansing when they are disobedient. This is how we can be established *blameless in holiness* ...' Today's church is not perfect. Far from it! But then, let us not forget the words of Edward Mote (1797-1874):

When he shall come with trumpet sound,
O may I then in him be found!
Clothed in his righteousness alone,
Faultless to stand before the throne.

In other words, for us to be acceptable to God in heaven, we must be accepted by God here on earth. There are three grounds for our acceptance:

- the Beloved – Jesus – in whom we are accepted (Ephesians 1:6)

- the belief – the gospel – through which we are accepted (1 Timothy 1:15)

- the behaviour – pleasing the Lord – by which we are accepted (2 Corinthians 5:9)

One day, one glorious morning, Paul's prayer will be finally answered, for we know that 'when he appears we shall be like him, because we shall see him as he is' (1 John 3:2). We shall be Jesus look-a-likes in eternity!

A Trinitarian feel

Paul's aspiration is unparalleled for the Trinity is involved in it. He addressed the Father and Son in verse 11. In verse 12 it is highly probable that *the Lord* refers to the Holy Spirit, since *our Lord* at the end of verse 13 specifically refers to Jesus Christ. If this is so, then this is the only prayer in the New Testament that is directed to the Holy Spirit! As we know, the normal pattern for prayer is to the Father, through the Son, and in the Holy Spirit. Since the Spirit is the sanctifier of the believer, and this is a prayer for sanctified, holy living, the address to the Spirit is proper and certainly not out of place.

Marks of a healthy gospel church

The essence of a good church is:

- knowing answered prayer

- getting on with the job in hand

- standing up and being counted for the Lord

- resolutely facing a myriad of troubles when they arise

- winning the battle against the enemy

- showing strength of character

- having stability in our personal commitment to Jesus

- keeping an eye on a future eternity

- believing the countdown to Christ's coming is getting lower every day

The outcome is inevitable: our faith will mature, our love will abound, and our lives will be holy. We are up to speed with current affairs and we look at events unfolding all around us through the lens of eternity. We are relevant! Paul, therefore, throws down the gauntlet and challenges us with three punchy statements:

- to grow wiser
- to grow stronger
- to grow purer

Mark #4

A church where hope is encouraged

While on a hazardous expedition to Antarctica and the South Pole, British explorer Sir Ernest Shackleton left a few men on Elephant Island, promising that he would return. Later, when he tried to go back, huge icebergs blocked the way. But suddenly, as if by a miracle, an avenue opened in the ice and Shackleton was able to get through.

His men, ready and waiting, quickly scrambled aboard. No sooner had the ship cleared the island than the ice crashed together behind them with an ear-splitting din. Contemplating their narrow escape, the ruddy explorer said to his men, 'It was fortunate you were all packed and ready to go!'

With one voice, they replied, 'Whenever the sea was clear of ice, we rolled up our sleeping bags and reminded each other that he may come today.'

4:1-2

In sixth gear

Have you heard the latest definition of an optimist? It is someone who believes the preacher is almost finished when he says, 'Finally!' From a purely statistical point of view, it is interesting to note that in chapters 1-3 there are a total of 43 verses, and in chapters 4-5 there are another 46 to add to the total. So the big question is: What does Paul really mean when he says, *finally*?

It is like a change of gear as he moves into overdrive. He ups the ante; he raises the stakes. The word could be better translated 'and now'. It is the punchline. A watershed. A transition. In a deft touch, Paul turns from narrative to exhortation, diverting attention from himself to them. This is the business end of his epistle where, as John Stott says, 'Paul moves from his apologia to his appeal.'

Having said that, Paul's sudden shift of theme does not mean that there are no tangible links between chapters 3 and 4. For one thing, his prayer that the Lord would cause them to grow in love and holiness (3:12-13) is what paves the way for his teaching about both issues in verses 3 and 9. Paul has given the young believers a crash course in Bible doctrine in chapters 1-3; in the following two chapters, he encourages them to let the rubber hit the road. They have learned all about it in terms of theory, now they need to go and live it out in the real world and prove to themselves that it does work. Doctrine is gripping stuff, it smacks of the Michelin syndrome!

Hitting the parade ground

The bottom line in our lives is that we should be walking in step with the Lord. To quote William Cowper, 'O for a closer walk with God.' In fact, that is a picture often painted in the word of God, and one that Paul uses over thirty-two times in his letters. For example, in Ephesians we are to 'walk in a manner worthy of the calling to which [we] have been called' (4:1) … 'walk in love' (5:2) … and 'walk as children of light' (5:8).

Why a walk? The Christian faith at that time was often called 'the Way' (Acts 9:2). What is more appropriate then than a walk along the Way? Paul's use of this particular term incorporates the idea that gospel people must not remain stationary.

- It demands life, for a dead sinner cannot walk.

- It entails growth, for a little baby cannot walk.

- It requires liberty, for someone who is bound cannot walk.

- It cries out for light, for very few of us want to go for a stroll in the dark.

- It cannot be hidden, for it is witnessed by all.

- It suggests progress towards a goal.

The Christian life begins with a step of faith and that single step should lead to a life of consistently walking by faith. There is no room for immobility. Paul says elsewhere that 'we live by faith, not by sight' (2 Corinthians 5:7, NIV). Such childlike faith is not a step into the dark, it is a leap forward into the light. How should we then walk? What is the trajectory your life is on? Paul leaves us in no doubt that we are to walk in:

- holiness (verses 1-8)
- harmony (verses 9-10)
- honesty (verses 11-12)
- hope (verses 13-18)

Walk on, with your head held high. Walk tall!

A man under God's thumb

Paul tells the church in these opening verses what God expects from them. His language is forthright, to say the least. Plain spoken. He pulls no punches. Paul's use of the word *instructions* is indicative of how seriously he feels about this entire matter. It is a word that was often used either for a military command or a civil order. It is a term more in keeping with a judicial setting, for it was frequently employed by magistrates at the bench in a court of law.

His impassioned concern and burden is that his friends in Thessalonica should strive for excellence in their Christian experience. So he reminds them of the will of God for their lives, a no-turning-back mindset that he wishes them to embrace. He desperately wants them to live a life that is pleasing to the Lord Jesus, a path of implicit obedience to the word of God. We adopt that outlook when we jubilantly walk in the ways of the Lord and are totally abandoned to him.

The fairly sketchy story of Enoch (the man we read about in the books of Genesis, Hebrews, and Jude) is relevant. We are not told much about him in Scripture, but one thing we do know is that he had a remarkably outstanding testimony in that it was said of him, 'he pleased God' (Hebrews 11:5).

Sometimes, human nature being what it is, we try to please ourselves. Maybe we fall into the trap of attempting to please other people. What really matters, more than anything else, is that we always seek to please the Lord. Paul could write, 'If I were still trying to please man, I would not be a servant of Christ' (Galatians 1:10). The inescapable fact is that he who tries to please everybody ends up pleasing nobody! Abraham Lincoln noted that 'you can please all of the people some of the time, and some of the people all of the time, but you can't please all of the people all of the time!' A quote from Eric Geiger says it all, 'If you want to make everyone happy, don't be a leader. Sell ice cream!'

Wallie Amos Criswell (1909-2002), former pastor of First Baptist Church, Dallas and two-times president of the Southern Baptist Convention, tells the story of a train master who was responsible for the smooth operation of a busy depot in the heart of a crowded city. A passer-by commended him for his obvious display of grace and tact as he juggled his many responsibilities, including answering various queries, giving directions, and maintaining the smooth operation of the depot. 'How do you do it?' the passer-by asked. 'With so many hurried people, disgruntled and angry ... how do you maintain your composure?' The train master replied, 'Why, it is no big deal. I do not have all these people to please. I only have to please just one man.' He pointed to an office and to a window on the second floor, and he said, 'My master sits in that office, and it is he alone that I have to please.'

4:3

Shades of sanctification

The six-million-dollar question is: How do we please the Lord? By doing the will of God. Simples. This is one of four key passages where Paul used a phrase like this, *For this is the will of God* – the others are: Ephesians 5:17, Colossians 1:9, and 1 Thessalonians 5:16-18. In a nutshell, there we have God's will for our lives. No 8-ball needed, no tarot cards needed, no palm reading needed. I love to stand in the pulpit and tell people: 'I know exactly what God's will is for your life.' After they have recovered from the initial shock of hearing such an audacious statement, I turn them to this verse. God's will is for you to be godly!

According to what Paul intimates in these verses, sanctification is God's perfect will for each of us. However, the minute we mention the S-word, people are often confused. Maybe it is not your thing. It is not hip to be holy, you think. Uncool, perhaps. They have a potpourri of weird, wonderful, and wacky ideas as to what it is and is not.

I wonder what the word 'holy' conveys to you? What pictures does it conjure up in your mind? I know it is funereally dismal to some, for they tend to associate it with no jokes, hair shirts, and freezing-cold showers. It is monastic to others who link it to a solitary, celibate lifestyle. The mental picture is of stone cells, no women or kids, and no Internet, Instagram or iPad. Kevin DeYoung writes in his book, *The Hole In Our Holiness*, that 'it's all too common to think of holiness as some sort of snooty do-goodism, prudish moralism, or ugly legalism.'

Some perceive it to be a kind of religious sheep-dip they are put through, a once-for-all experience of cleansing and commitment. Once they have been dipped or 'done', they think everything is fine, hunky-dory from then on in. Other folk see sanctification as an extraction process whereby God uses a supernatural magnet to remove all sin from their lives, and from that moment on, they have no trouble pleasing the Lord. Easy-peasy. Nothing could be further from the truth!

Relationships

In the Bible, holiness is intensely practical. It is concerned with daily living in the home and relationships in the church and wider community. We cannot be holy by ourselves. There are no shortcuts. It takes time – lots of time – to be holy. It is primarily concerned with relationships, and it seems to me that there are four areas involved:

- the relationship between an individual and God
- the relationship between men and women
- the relationship between one Christian and another Christian

- the relationship between a Christian and his neighbour

In other words, holiness has to be meticulously worked out in our marriage, in the context of our local gospel church, and it has to be evidenced in our place of regular employment. Paul states quite categorically that if we cannot be holy in the daily, routine business of life, opting for seclusion in a monastery in the back of beyond will not help us.

The reality is that holiness has not had a particularly good press in recent times. It is often a nonstarter with the average person, who views it as heavy on finger-pointing and embarrassingly out-of-touch. People, for reasons best known to themselves, are turned off by it. They see so-called holy people as those who have been soaked in embalming fluid, dour and dull with the uncanny knack of frowning on anything that smacks of hilarious fun or pleasure. But God has other ideas, for holiness of life is the gold standard.

Beautiful people

The Old Testament speaks about the 'beauty of holiness' (Psalm 96:9) in that there is an exquisite loveliness associated with it. Matthew Henry is on the ball when he notes that 'the beauty of holiness needs no paint.' There is something stunningly attractive about a life lived the way God intended. 'God is in the beautification business,' writes Kevin DeYoung. This means that God is designing beautiful people, not merely on the outside, but on the inside; he is washing away spots and smoothing out wrinkles. People who are admirable, trustworthy, strong, loving, and compassionate – people who are whole. That is, people who are holy. The only explanation for their enhanced quality of life is that they are sanctified.

This is the old-time religion of the clean life and pure heart. Something incredibly positive. It means we are monopolised by the Lord, we cleave and cling to him and his precepts, we are exclusively for the Master's use. It is when we turn our back on sin and sensual pleasures; it is when we leave the world behind and burn all our bridges.

Here is the key that unlocks the door to a deeper spiritual life, leading us to a new dimension of Christian living. It enables us to scale new heights with the Lord. Here is life beyond the higher plane, on the highest plateau, a sanctified life. Basically, it means we are set apart *by* him, *for* him, and *unto* him. Even after God has declared us righteous, his next step is to make us righteous; such is sanctification. As the author of *Knowing God*, J I Packer put it, 'In reality, holiness is the goal of our redemption. As Christ died in order that we may be justified, so we are justified in order that we may be sanctified and made holy.'

This is the heart of Old Testament theology, where we read that the Sabbath was sanctified as a special, one-in-seven day of rest (Leviticus 23:3). The tabernacle in the desert and the temple in Jerusalem were both sanctified, as they were set apart by God's immanent presence (Exodus 40:34-35; 2 Chronicles 7:1-3). God sanctified the nation of Israel as his own treasured possession (Deuteronomy 7:6), and he sanctified the sons of Levi to serve in his courts in a priestly ministry (Deuteronomy 10:8).

The triple P

Sanctification is strangely similar to our salvation in that it is in three distinct tenses: we have been saved, we are being saved, and one day we shall be saved. We also declare that we have been sanctified in the past; we are being sanctified in the present; and we shall be sanctified in the future. Therefore, sanctified is what we are and what we must become.

Yesterday, we were set apart from the penalty of sin. That is positional in nature. Some theologians call this gift of holiness through union with Christ our 'definitive sanctification'. It is what happened at the moment we trusted in Jesus Christ as our Lord and Saviour. Today, we are being set apart from the power of sin. This is progressive in that it is an ongoing-for-your-whole-life process. In that sense, it is gradual. Tomorrow, in God's timing, we shall be set apart from the presence of sin. This is perpetual for we read, 'See what kind of love the Father has given to us, that we should be called children of God; and so we are … Beloved, we are God's children now, and what we will be has not yet appeared; but we know what when he appears we shall be like him, because we shall see him as he is' (1 John 3:1-2).

Sanctification is a continuous process, not a hit-or-miss goal, of growing closer to Christ! It begins for us in a new nature, with our conversion to faith in Christ on earth, and it ends for us in a new body, face-to-face with Christ in heaven.

- We look back and say, Christ *for* me.
- We reflect on the present and say, Christ *in* me.
- We look forward with anticipation to the future and say, Christ *with* me.

All for one, one for all

The word *sanctified* is almost the same as the word 'holiness' in that they both come from the same root. The ethos and heartbeat of sanctification is that the Lord has set apart the one that is godly for himself (Psalm 4:3). With that thought in mind, it is fascinating to discover that the Trinity plays a major part in our sanctification. Jude 1 reminds us that the Father decrees it in his sovereign purpose and plan. Hebrews 13:12 tells us that the Son determines it because this is one of the benefits of the atonement. Romans 15:16 indicates that the Holy Spirit directs it through the application of the word of God to our lives.

A similar note is struck in John 17:17-19 where the Saviour prayed in his high-priestly prayer in the upper room, 'Sanctify them by the truth, your word is truth.' The word of God is the agent of sanctification. As we read Scripture and hear it ministered, it has a cleansing effect on our lives: it meets our need, it shows up the spots and stains, it reveals all the blemishes, for we see ourselves as God sees us. Then, as we allow the water of the word to wash and purify us, we shall become more holy and more like Jesus. This great ministry of sanctification, therefore, implies cleansing. The Lord is looking for clean vessels and the only way to do that is for us to mortify the old nature and feed the new man (*cf.* Paul's teaching in Romans 6-7).

It suggests commissioning, for in Christ we are gospel-driven vessels designed for higher service. We are sanctified so that he might send us out into a lost world with the message of eternal, redeeming love. We should also be practising our position in Christ, as it reflects a Christlikeness in our character. It is only when we know our position *in* Jesus that we can begin to live *like* Jesus. In other words, we should be holy within and without, just like him. As David Peterson puts it, 'Believers are definitively consecrated to God in order to live dedicated and holy lives, to his glory.'

Holy or holey

To be sanctified is to live like a saint. Contrary to church law, saints are not those who have been canonised, but those who have been called by God and cleansed by his Son's precious blood. They are not those set in stained glass in a Gothic cathedral window, but those living in today's world in a pagan culture. A girl who attended worship in a place with a lot of stained-glass windows was asked what a saint was. 'A saint is a person the light shines through,' she replied. Every Christian is a saint and every saint is a Christian.

All of this is a matter for the heart, and the heart of the matter is our personal holiness. That was ever the supreme concern of Robert Murray McCheyne, the nineteenth-century pastor of St Peter's Church in Dundee, who often said, 'My people's greatest need is my personal holiness.' He went on to say that 'we are as holy as we choose to be.' I do not know what impact that has on your heart, but I find it enormously challenging. In moments like these, George Jackson's (1866-93) hymn says it so eloquently:

I want, dear Lord,
A heart that's true and clean;
A sunlit heart, with not a cloud between;
A heart like thine, a heart divine,
A heart as white as snow;
On me, dear Lord,
A heart like this bestow.

Reality check

God is much more interested in our character than in the career we pursue, in who we are than in what we do. One of the tell-tale signs of a deteriorating society is a loss of moral integrity. When this foundation stone begins to crack and erode, the effect is nothing short of disastrous. That is where Christianity has been outstandingly different from day one. God's people have vigorously campaigned against moral decline by upholding personal holiness. Down the years of church history, gospel people have been committed to purity of heart and life, in spite of prevailing winds and many siren voices clamouring for their attention. They have dug in their stilettos and obstinately stood their ground.

Why have so many of God's people remained resolute and defiant? The only explanation is found in these verses. It would be so easy for us to look around and wring our clammy hands and bemoan our lot. Sometimes we say, it has never been so bad before! The fact of the matter is, there is nothing new under the sun and what is happening across the world today is certainly not a last-days phenomenon.

All the more reason why we need to be the kind of people Paul is talking about in this chapter. In a grim and dirty world, we should be abandoned to Jesus Christ. We should be like the men of Isaachar and know what is happening on our front doorstep (1 Chronicles 12:32). This is the emphatic challenge we face in the third millennium. There is a patent need for us to be different and stand out in the crowd. We must be! We dare to be! We should be men and women who unashamedly quick march under the unfurled banner of holiness. Lelia Naylor Morris (1862-1929) rallies each of us as squaddies in God's army with these stirring words:

Called unto holiness, children of light,
Walking with Jesus in garments of white;
Raiment unsullied, nor tarnished with sin,
God's Holy Spirit abiding within.

'Holiness to the Lord,' is our watchword and song,
'Holiness to the Lord,' as we're marching along:
Sing it, shout it, loud and long,
'Holiness to the Lord,' now and for ever.

4:3b-5

Straight talk about sex

When unbelievers look at us, they should see lives that are attractive and beautiful, for we are numbered among those who know and love the Lord. It is in that context that Paul moves on to talk about something of mega importance to all people in every generation. He addresses the prickly subject of our relationship with members of the opposite sex. Vintage Paul, he handles it tenderly and tactfully. He deals sensitively with the subject of sex.

At the same time, there is a toughness to his approach when he reminds them of the serious consequences of disobeying the word of God. It is straight talk about moral purity. Insight for Living broadcaster Charles Swindoll says, 'Here we have grass-stained advice from someone following Christ in the grassroots of life.'

It is a fair assumption to make that these words are rarely preached on. They are not very high in the popularity ratings for selecting as our favourite Bible portion, definitely not in the top three, never mind the top ten. And yet they are exceedingly relevant in a post-Christian, postmodern era.

We live in a grossly immoral society where anything, and I mean anything, goes. The standards of acceptable behaviour have plummeted to an all-time low. We are on a downward spiral, teetering on the brink of disaster. We have gone full circle. We are living dangerously, as we have returned to the days of Noah and Lot. It is indubitably obvious that we live in a sex-mad culture. This world is sex-saturated.

John MacArthur writes, 'We live in a culture that is indulging itself in every conceivable and inconceivable sexual activity.' Not only is sexual sin tolerated in any form by any one with anyone else at any time, in any place, in any way; more than that, it is advocated, promoted, encouraged, and aggressively marketed through every media we can possibly think of, on the basis of freedom of speech … but whose freedom?

There is so much innuendo in the 60-second advertising campaigns shown in the frequent commercial breaks on our television screens. What do scantily clad, blonde beauties have to do with selling fast cars, fast food, or fast computers? It does not matter which way we turn, we are constantly bombarded and blitzed by it. It is no accident that pornography is a fifty-billion-dollar industry. Sex sells, and a lot of people are buying it. Because of that, many vital issues are blurred in the almost impenetrable moral fog so prevalent at this moment.

Ann Widdecombe MP, speaking about the state of society in 2000, said, 'Let's face it, we are not a happier society as a result of the liberalisation of the seventies. We have record rates of divorce, record rates of suicide, record rates of teenage pregnancy, record rates of youth crime, record rates of underage sex. We should invite people to recognise that the Great Experiment has failed. You cannot have happiness without restraint.'

Power of purity

This is an hour of enormous need, and the great need of

the hour is for gospel people to maintain moral purity. Paul here is gutsy, but he is honest and sincere to the core as he probes into the nerve centre of our lives. He is right on target as he pinpoints the very things that cry out for immediate attention, because it is the practice of purity which causes us to stand out from the world like a glistening diamond versus coal.

We are saints, we are sanctified, we are called to live separated lives unto the Lord, we are told to be different from the world, and we are exhorted to be a holy people. All this can only mean that God is looking for those who are sanctified 'through and through' (1 Thessalonians 5:23), because 'purity is the end of our election' (Thomas Watson).

- purity of life
- purity of heart
- purity of mind

This is for all of us. Fundamentally, a thrice-holy Lord is looking for the younger set to flee youthful passions (2 Timothy 2:22). He is looking for middle-aged folk to show by their lifestyle and behaviour that God's way is the best way. He is looking for seniors to set a superb example of godliness and real contentment. As Kevin DeYoung emphasises, 'God doesn't ask us to get familiar with sexual immorality on the big screen, TV screen, or smart phone screen so that we can engage the culture.' Because, in the words of Thomas Brooks (1608-80), 'A holy heart is always attended with a holy life.'

Sex and sanctification

In one inspirational breath, Paul declares, *For this is the will of God, your sanctification*, and in the very next breath, he says, *that you abstain from sexual immorality*. Whether we realise it or not, sanctification radically affects every department of life. It is like an antivirus programme operating in the background for each of us, protecting internal vulnerabilities against external threats.

Paul's teaching here is clear and distinct. He tells it like it is. There is no shilly-shallying. Alistair Begg makes the point that 'the plain things are the main things, and the main things are the plain things.' The Christian, therefore, should have nothing to do with anything which has an immorality label attached to it. There is no escape hatch or bolthole that we can squeeze through. He calls for a clean cut with everything that smacks of licentiousness. He makes an earnest plea for us to be at odds with society.

The Thessalonian problem is not dissimilar to that which faced the church in Corinth: a sexually-oriented and sexually-explicit community, a culture riddled and renowned for hard porn and sexual vice. But, Paul says, in spite of your cultural habits, old patterns, and former lifestyle, the Lord does not hack sexual sin. He never has done! He never will do! The baseline is this: the church of Jesus Christ cannot live like the devil's promiscuous world.

So far as Scripture is concerned, this is not a relative morality, it is an absolute standard. A blue ribbon, biblical standard. No matter how much the world tries to squeeze us into its mould, this divine standard does not change nor does it fluctuate. It is not raised or lowered depending on the direction of the prevailing wind.

We need to be clear that it is not just the act that Paul is thinking about, it is the attitude as well. The old adage holds true: if you play with fire, you will get badly burned. We should avoid it like the plague. It is doing what Joseph did when Potiphar's wife tried to lure him into an Egyptian cotton-sheeted bed. The minute he saw her coming down Petticoat Lane, he ran a mile as fast as his legs would carry him in the opposite direction (Genesis 39:7-12).

Saying 'no' to intimacy

Let me spell it out clearly so that we are left in absolutely no doubt as to what Paul is teaching. It means:

- no sexual wrongdoing whatsoever

- no fooling around on the back seat of a car

- no premarital sex even though we may be committed to a long-term, loving relationship with that person

- no messing around with someone else's partner because we are fed up and bored with our own

- no same-sex relationships

- no hard or soft porn from salacious books or glossy magazines that we find on the top shelf of the newspaper stand or when surfing the Internet

- no visiting highly dubious chat rooms online or telling smutty stories

- no entrance to strip clubs (and such like) or entertaining even the thought of using a prostitute

- no sitting up late to watch risqué movies on television or iPad

Paul's directive is calculatingly blunt and without apology. He says, 'Have none of these things going on in your life.' It is a blanket ban! I appreciate the way J B Phillips translates verse 3, 'God's plan is to make you holy, and that entails first of all, a clean break with sexual immorality.'

Self-control

Allied to that challenge is an overwhelming sense of privilege. We should be in charge of our own body, and when we are, God is glorified. That is what Paul says in verse 4, *that each one of you know how to control his own body in holiness and honour*. This is a skill we have to learn, as it does not come naturally or easily. It is not something that someone else can do for you; you have to do it yourself! I cannot pass the buck and blame the other person. The underlying thought is that I am solely responsible for my own actions.

It is a lesson we must learn if we are to grow spiritually and if our lives are to count for the Lord. We need to gain the mastery over our body so that we do not become slaves to our lusts. We need to know victory over the flesh and send the enemy running when he would seek to seduce us and tempt us. We are in a battle. The conflict is internal. The world is against us. The flesh is easy meat for the devil. As John MacArthur says, 'It is your unredeemed human flesh that is the beachhead to sin,' hence the Pauline injunction to *control* it.

There is a link here to Paul's comment in 1 Corinthians 6:12-20 where he is on a similar wavelength, and also to his insights in Galatians 5:16-26. The key to controlling our body is the Holy Spirit. If we walk in the Spirit, we will not fulfil the lusts of the flesh! Ah, that is what Paul says in verse 4! So the key to controlling our body is walking in the Spirit. The key to walking in the Spirit is being filled with the Spirit (Ephesians 5:18). And the key to being filled with the Spirit is letting God's word dwell in us richly (Colossians 3:16). As always, the focus is on our relationship with Jesus Christ.

Staying away from the edge

Paul is talking here about self-discipline, for purity is a conscious choice, it does not just happen. At the end of the verse, Paul reminds us of the degree to which this control is to be exercised. It is to be in *holiness and honour*. To live in *holiness* means to be separated unto God from sin and unto purity. To live in *honour* means to be worthy of respect. In other words, our body is to be so separated from sin that it clearly shows respect toward the God who owns it, who dwells in it, and whom it represents; and toward the church of which it is a part.

That sends a clear signal which says that we should live our lives without asking how far can we go without going over the line, but rather asking how far we can stay away and be utterly set apart from sin, honouring our body, which is God's, and using it for the glory of Christ.

A wrong kind of passion

Paul focuses on the peril when he writes, *not in the passion of lust like the Gentiles who do not know God*. What a strong indictment that is! *Passion of lust* is an incredibly powerful term! Either word is strong enough, but when we put them both together, it reinforces all that Paul is saying.

The word *passion* means an excited emotion, an uncontrollable desire, compelling feelings and overpowering urges. It is used here in a bad sense (*cf.* Romans 1:26; Colossians 3:5). The word for *lust* is an out-of-control craving. According to Frederick Buechner, it is 'the craving for salt of a man who is dying of thirst'. This is what happens when people sink to abject depths of crass immorality.

We are encouraged to look at the activities of the pagan population milling around us and see how they operate. Paul leaves no stone unturned when he says that their lives are governed by lust, they are controlled by their passions, they are ruled by sensual desire, and they live according to the dictates and demands of the flesh. In the final analysis, they do not know the Lord Jesus Christ since they have never entered into a personal, dynamic relationship with the living God.

Again, Paul reckons we should be different, for we know the Lord. God is a reality in our lives. Therefore, in terms of moral behaviour, we should be an example. We should be setting the tone of every conversation; we should be seen to be above and beyond reproach in the wider community; we should exercise utmost care and caution in the programmes we watch on television or at the theatre; we need to be highly selective in what we allow our eyes to focus and feast upon. That inevitably means some stuff will be classed as out of bounds for one who is sensitive to the person of the Holy Spirit.

If we fantasise and tantalise ourselves with sin, we end up morally and spiritually weakened. Massively so. The omens are not good: remember the fateful, one-night stand in 2 Samuel 11 of David and Bathsheba! That means from Paul's incisive teaching in verse 5 that we must not ignore the flashing warning lights. The man is an idiot who drives through a red light! So is the man who speeds up when he sees an amber caution! We must be ultra-careful for it is the glory of Christ that is at stake. Because of who we are in Christ, we need to set a good and godly example to all those around us.

4:6

When 'no' means 'no'

Ethics are important, and core values are essential, we cannot live or do without them. What we believe determines the way we behave! One impacts the other. It is apparent that such a principle undergirds every aspect of life. It holds equally true when it comes to dealing with the often tangled emotional web of interpersonal relationships, especially those we enjoy with the opposite sex.

It is a thorny patch we are walking on in this section, but we cannot avoid it, as Paul talks about a divine prohibition. He really lays it on the line as to what weighs heavily on the mind and heart of God. We are left in no doubt as to what the Lord thinks about the entire scenario, for Paul writes, *that no one transgress and wrong his brother in this matter*.

When a man commits fornication and/or engages in adultery, the ramifications are huge, as it affects so many innocent lives to a greater or lesser extent. The upshot is often immeasurable and the damage incalculable. Adultery is where inclination meets opportunity. It takes two to tango outside of God's will. Sexual immorality hurts both parties in one way or another, the one doing the lusting and the one being lusted after. Having said that, we can narrow the issue down and say it has primarily a twofold effect:

One, the offender does wrong in that he seriously oversteps the mark: he goes beyond the boundary, he goes too far, he exceeds the limits, he goes over the line; and in so doing, violates another person's body. Consequently, he transgresses.

Two, when the person commits such a blatant sin, he takes advantage of the other person. He is only thinking about himself and his personal gratification, a momentary thrill. To all intents and purposes, such a person is guilty of fraud. He wants something that does not belong to him and he goes for something that is not his. An individual who rides recklessly down this path is covetous and falls foul of the avarice and selfish greed of his heart. He has ruthlessly asserted himself on another individual, and is therefore guilty of cheating. He leaves behind him a trail of broken hearts, a long line of broken lives, and a string of broken promises and vows.

This is unbelievably strong language that Paul employs. And yet, when we sit down and hear what God says, we know it is true to life, and we also know that it makes an awful lot of good sense.

Man ... he's my brother

Paul's use of the word *brother* is most illuminating. This is the only time the inspired apostle uses this particular Greek word. It means not only a brother in the Christian family, as it goes far beyond the confines of that, for it also includes our fellow man. In other words, it is not exclusive to the people of God. It is all-inclusive, for no person made in the image of God is omitted, and it is all-embracing, for no one person in the world is excluded. The implication is that this kind of behaviour is not acceptable, it never has been acceptable, and no matter how we dress it up, it never can be acceptable. It is never viewed as the norm in the eyes of the Lord, and because of that, we can never justify it.

What are the consequences of such grossly outrageous behaviour? Paul says that *the Lord is an avenger in all these things*. People are inclined to forget that God sees what goes on under the duvet in the nation's bedrooms. When the soft light is switched off, the Lord is not left in the dark. Biblically, sin is always associated with the dark, and holiness is always associated with light. It is much better to see where we are going!

John MacArthur writes that 'sexual sin disregards God, it ignores his holiness, it spurns his will, it defies his commands, it rejects his love, it flaunts his grace, it abuses his mercy. It is disobedient, it is selfish, it is ingratitude, and God will avenge it.'

Sooner or later it will catch us up; it will come back to terrorise and haunt us. We cannot hide from God in time, and we certainly cannot run away from him in eternity. We need to get this straight, whether we like it or not, there is definitely coming a day of accountability, a day of reckoning when all will be revealed. God sees all things, he knows all that happens, and all impurity, he will judge.

Cause and effect

If any one of us happens to fall in this way, the good news is that there is forgiveness with the Lord if we genuinely seek him in repentance. Although failure is never final, our repentance had better be genuine. Constantly going back to the well for forgiveness without meaning it, is libertine. Sure, the Lord will forgive our sin, which says a lot about his marvellous mercy and generous grace; but, understand this, we will have to live with the serious repercussions of such a disastrous step for the rest of our lives. Given time, there may be a measure of healing; the odds are, the scars will always remain.

That is one of the prime reasons why, regarding matters of leadership in a gospel church, Paul writes to young Timothy in the manner he does. He makes no bones about it when he declares that such men, i.e. elders and deacons, should be 'the husband of one wife' (1 Timothy 3:2). The same high standard is still appropriate today for all those involved in any kind of Christian leadership in church and mission. It is an interesting turn of phrase, for it not only means that he is married to one woman at a given point in time, it essentially means that he is a one-woman man.

Some folk prefer to give it a different name, but at the end of the day, sin is sin. Someone severely criticised their pastor on one occasion for preaching against sin in the life of the Christian. They felt that sin in the life of a believer was different from sin in the life of an unconverted person. The godly pastor thought for a few minutes, then he said, 'Yes, you're right, it's worse!'

God will never condemn sin in a sinner, and at the same time, condone it in the life of any one of his children, even though he will still forgive us if we genuinely repent. It is true that there is no condemnation for those who are in Christ Jesus (Romans 8:1), but that does not mean God will gloss over all our shortcomings when we stray into sin's bypath meadow. In Christ he overlooks our sins in a judicial sense, however he is not blind to them. Bishop John Charles Ryle (1816-1900) of Liverpool said, 'We must not expect sin, excite sin, or excuse sin.'

4:7

Sunshine in the soul

Paul challenges us to keep the whole issue in perspective by looking at it from an eternal vantage point, *For God has not called us for impurity, but in holiness.* This is the rationale behind Paul's sweeping instruction in the previous verse. It puts the spotlight back on the exalted Lord. God has called each of us to a life of holiness, or what could be termed, a life of wholeness. He wants us to move out of the fog of our impurity into the bright light of his holiness.

That is why he saved us, redeemed us, chose us, and cleansed us. His ultimate goal is that we might be a holy people. His aspiration for us is that we might be like Jesus. His dream for us is that we might reflect his Son through our lives having been washed in his precious blood. He longs that we might be vessels unto honour that will glorify him (2 Timothy 2:21).

4:8

Flouting God's law

This immensely challenging section concludes with Paul speaking about our profession, when he says, *Therefore whoever disregards this, disregards not man but God, who gives his Holy Spirit to you*. This phrase is like a sign saying, 'Trespassers Will Be Prosecuted.' Paul says, if you do not listen to what I am telling you, it is not me you are rejecting, it is not the elders you are ignoring, it is not your friends and family you are opposing, it is the Lord that you are standing against.

The fornicator and adulterer is someone who flatly rejects God, not man. The individual who does that is in a sad and sorry state; he is backing a loser all the way. Richard Mayhue crystallises Paul's thinking when he writes, 'The one who continues to live immorally rejects God's Spirit, rejects God's will, rejects God's call, rejects God's word, and rejects God's pleasure. To put it simply, they reject God.'

A closer reading of this verse indicates that there are three basic steps to a life of holiness. We need to:

- recognise his presence – we have been given the Spirit of God and he abides within
- respect his person – he is the Holy Spirit
- receive his power – for he alone can make us holy

The stark choice, the simple choice, is ours. We can look at it like this: Do we live our lives on a horizontal plane in the weakness of the flesh, or do we live our lives vertically in the dynamic and power of the Holy Spirit? As Robert Murray McCheyne used to say, 'A holy man is an awesome weapon in the hand of God.' Paul is making an impassioned plea for purity in these verses so that we might be enabled and energised by him to live for Jesus in a world that is rotten to the core. What a rousing challenge for us to live for God in a sex-mad society. To quote Charles Swindoll, 'Purity involves more than a passing glance to see how much dirt we have under our fingernails. It requires a good, soaped up, scrubbed down Saturday night bath.'

4:9-10

Philadelphia – not cheese, but love

Now concerning brotherly love you have no need for anyone to write to you, for you yourselves have been taught by God to love one another, for that indeed is what you are doing to all the brothers throughout Macedonia. But we urge you, brothers, to do this more and more.

We feel the change of atmosphere when Paul moves from chastity to charity; there is a distinctly different tone in these verses. He says, 'I want to talk to you guys about brotherly love.' This should be the hallmark of every Christian. Our trademark. He wants us to abound in affection.

General William Westmoreland was once reviewing a platoon of paratroopers in Vietnam. As he went down the line, he asked each of them a question: 'How do you like jumping, son?'

'Love it, sir!' was the first answer.

'How do you like jumping?' he asked the next.

'The greatest experience in my life, sir!' exclaimed the ebullient paratrooper.

'How do you like jumping?' he asked the third.

'I hate it, sir,' he replied.

'Then why do you do it?' asked the bemused Westmoreland.

'Because I want to be around guys who love to jump!'

The brand of love that Paul refers to is *philadelphia* love, the love that binds our hearts together. We are the children of God, brothers and sisters in the global family of God. He is our Father, and he is love. In other words, the more we live like God in a life of purity, the more we love one another. It is a love of deep affection that brings us out of our ivory theological towers to get involved in helping others who are struggling in the trenches of life.

It is a family love, for we have kindred hearts and minds, as we share something in common. Like the paratrooper, we enjoy being around those who love to jump! The ground is level at Calvary. It was said of those in the first-century church, 'See how they love each other.' It is a fragrant love, for when there is love shared among us, there is a pervasive richness and a sense of wonder in the atmosphere. We can tell a mile away if people love one another, and we can also tell if people are getting on one another's nerves.

It is a fruitful love, for we want nothing but the best for others; we want to see Christ shining from their lives; and we want to discern the glory of God in all that we do together in his name.

Love one another

Paul says they were *taught by God*, which seems quite remarkable. J Ligon Duncan says that 'in the original it is one Greek word and apparently Paul invented it. He took the word "God" and the word "taught" and he stuck them together to say they were God-taught. We think he invented the word because we can't find any example of it in ancient Greek literature prior to Paul and only a few people use it after Paul.'

God not only teaches us about love, but he also teaches us how to love. That is how they were able to do it. It was the work of God in their hearts. It was an operation of the Holy Spirit deep down within.

- God the Father taught us by example when he gave the Lord Jesus to die for us (Romans 5:8).

- God the Son taught us when he said, 'A new commandment I give unto you, that you love one another' (John 13:34).

- God the Holy Spirit taught us when he poured the love of God into our hearts when we trusted Christ (Romans 5:5).

We are to show love to all the brethren, without exception. None are left out and none should feel excluded in any way. Not easy, sometimes. It goes against the grain at other times. The ditty is right when it says:

To dwell above with saints in love,
That will indeed be glory,
To dwell below with saints we know,
Well, that's another story.

Sometimes we hurt each other by the comments that we make and by the things that we do, or perhaps, do not say or do. There are just some people who are easy to get along with, people with whom we have an instant rapport; then there are others who rub us up the wrong way and tramp on our toes, usually those with corns or calluses. There are some folk with whom we hit it off, and others whom we feel like hitting! We have an easy relationship with some; it is more strained with others. Some of God's wonderful people are touchy-feely; others are tetchy and keep us at arm's length.

We have our own ideas, our differences of opinion, our peculiarities, it is just that some are more eccentric than others. We are as different as chalk and cheese. But, says Paul, it does not matter what we are like, we can still love each other. Love ultimately wins the day, no matter how long it takes. Love overcomes the whole gamut of problems. Love goes beyond the jarring clash of personalities and cultures. Love gladly accepts the other person, for who and what they are. Love always finds a way through the maze of complex issues. Love does exactly what it says on the tin – it loves!

Touching people's lives

What does Paul have to say about the expression of such love? We discover that their love was well known throughout the whole of Macedonia. As Mark Howell notes, 'Our love for *our* church is not enough; we must love *God's* church.' How did they do it? It appears that one of the most obvious ways was through the engaging ministry of hospitality. Open hearts, open homes, for love is the hinge on which hospitality turns to open its unlocked door.

From Hebrews 13:1-3 we are exhorted to show hospitality to three kinds of people – saints, strangers, and those who are suffering. Paul was all too aware that they were loving many different types of people, but he urged them to keep it up. They were not to pause and mark time, or even maintain the status quo. He wants them to go out and break new ground for the Lord; he wants them to expand their love, to reach out more and more. We can never get too much love, and we can never give too much love.

4:11-12

To be honest with you

Having given them a lecture on love, Paul moves on to give them some instructions on integrity; that is, walking in honesty. The opening phrase – *to aspire to* – is an encouragement and an incentive to them to be ambitious (see NIV translation). There is nothing inherently wrong with healthy ambition or godly aspiration, it all depends what it is focused upon. Is it popularity, power, position, or prestige? If it is, we are barking up the wrong tree.

Paul uses this same word *aspire* three times in the New Testament. In Romans 15:20 it was his all-consuming passion to reach the unreached with the message of Jesus and his love; he wanted to tell the gospel to the untold millions. Again, we come across it in 2 Corinthians 5:9 where his sincerely-held desire is that in everything he might please the Lord Jesus. And also here, where it is a threefold ambition, for we are *to live quietly, and to mind [our] own affairs, and to work with [our] hands*. What does he mean by each of these?

- Do not irritate!

To live quietly is to be tranquil on the inside. It is not what we see advertised in the tabloid press when they encourage us to pay a visit to the local health shop to buy a bottle of tablets designed to give us perfect peace. It is not the hermit mentality either. It is living on the ragged edge with a peace in our hearts and minds. Contentment. A life that is free from anger, conflict, and hostility. It is when we feel relaxed in God's love, because we rest in his care. It is all about learning to lean on the everlasting arms of the Lord Jesus. This rich quality is found as we intentionally wait upon the Lord. Others will see the Lord through our actions.

- Do not interfere!

Paul bluntly tells them not to meddle in other people's affairs (2 Thessalonians 3:11-12). They are to keep their noses clean and not barge into situations unless first invited. They must not gatecrash another man's privacy. One translation says, 'Do not be a busybody.' Elizabeth Elliot has a timely instruction for us all, when she writes, 'Never pass up the opportunity to keep your mouth shut.' This applies to every aspect of life – in the church, in the local community, in business and, certainly, in the family. Potentially, we would save ourselves a lot of peeved aggravation if we took this to heart.

- Do not idle!

There is no virtue in living like a parasite or a moocher. If we have a job to do, we thank God for it, and get on with it. Do not be a time-waster. We should use every moment God has allocated to us and invest it wisely for him. Antonio Stradivari (1644-1737), the great maker of violins, said, 'If my hand slacked, I should rob God.' 'Why bother working?' is the all-important question. John Stott makes the point that 'the idle are unwilling, not unable, to work.' As the old saying goes, the devil finds work for idle hands to do. 'An idle person,' writes Thomas Watson, 'is the devil's tennis ball which he bandies up and down with temptation till at last the ball goes out of play.' It was Mark Twain who said, 'I do not like work, even when someone else does it.' Honesty is not the best policy for the Christian, it is the only one. That is supremely the reason why we need to be men and women of aspirational ambition.

Impacting our world

Since the world is watching, Paul exhorts us to *walk properly before outsiders and be dependent on no one*. The unconverted are looking at our lives. And they miss nothing! They see us and they know us. If we are the kind of people that God wants us to be, then the man next door will respect us for who and what we are. In other words, we shall bear a good testimony.

Remember Enoch, for that is how he operated. If ever there was one, here was a man who walked with God, who pleased God and who, when he was gone to heaven, was really missed. People in the neighbourhood were genuinely sorry to see him go, such was his positive influence. Ron Hutchcraft tells the story of meeting a woman from his church. Upon greeting her, he asked, 'What do you do for a living?' With a huge grin, she replied, 'Pastor, I'm a disciple of Jesus Christ – cleverly disguised as a machine operator!' That woman clearly understood that her faith meant something. She got it.

What a stimulating challenge for us to live so as to be missed and to live so that Christ will be magnified. Sure, we may be out of step with the world, but we are in tune with the Lord and in touch with the Lord. We should live so that when the final summons comes, we shall leave something more behind us than an epitaph on a headstone or an obituary in a local newspaper. Will Rogers encourages us to 'so live that we wouldn't be ashamed to sell the family parrot to the town gossip!' We should live so that the pastor can tell the truth at our funeral! To me, that is what a real gospel person is all about!

4:13

Sound theology

I love the *Peanuts* cartoons. One of my favourites is the one that involves a fairly intense conversation between Lucy and Linus. Looking out a window, Lucy wonders, 'Boy, look at it rain … what if it floods the whole world?' 'It will never do that,' says Linus, with real conviction in his voice. 'You see, in Genesis 9 God promised Noah that would never happen again, and the sign of the promise is the rainbow.' 'You've taken a great load off my mind,' replies Lucy, to whom Linus responds, 'Sound theology has a way of doing that!' That is precisely what Paul offers in these verses!

- the practical results of Christianity (verses 1-12)
- the personal return of Christ (verses 13-18)

What we have here is a twofold picture: a gospel church energised in the Spirit, the people of God radiating holiness; and a gospel church expectant in the world, the people of God reflecting hope and living in keen anticipation of the second advent of Jesus.

The next major world event is the return of Jesus Christ. Statisticians tell us there are 1,845 Old Testament references to the second coming of Christ, with a total of 17 books out of a possible 39 giving it eminence. When we move across to the New Testament, the figures are no less impressive. For example, of the 260 chapters in the New Testament there is a minimum 318 references to the second advent. That averages 1 out of every 30 verses dedicated to this cherished truth. By any stretch of the imagination that is quite staggering. When we probe a bit further, we discover that 23 of the 27 New Testament books refer to the subject of the Lord's return. Three of these books are one-chapter letters written to specific persons on a single subject. For every prophecy of the first coming of Christ when he was born as a babe in Bethlehem, there are eight prophecies of his second coming. That tells me that this truth is central to the word of God. Alistair Begg affirms that 'the return of Jesus Christ is an absolute certainty. It will be personal, visible, cosmic, and glorious.'

Living well, dying well

This is a chapter of truly remarkable contrasts, such as:

- life *vis-à-vis* death
- here and now *vis-à-vis* there and then

- thoughts on time *vis-à-vis* exploring eternity
- those wide awake *vis-à-vis* those fallen asleep

Basically, Paul is talking about living well and dying well. To die well, to die with dignity, means we embrace a wonderful hope that looks forward to a better day when we shall see the King in his unerring beauty. Charles Wesley's splendid words reflect this princely attitude:

Happy, if with my latest breath
I may but gasp his name;
Preach him to all, and cry in death,
'Behold, behold the Lamb!'

Hope in a no-hope world

Hope is just what postmodern man is searching for; the trouble is, unlike Job, he often looks in the wrong place. He asked the double-barrelled question: 'Where then is my hope? Who will see my hope?' (Job 17:15).

When we see what is happening all around us in today's world we could easily be driven to the precarious edge of despair. Man's cherished dreams have not been fulfilled; his ideals have not been realised; his best-laid plans have been shattered. There are times when our backs are pinned to the wall, when we have that awful sinking feeling in the pit of our stomach, when we feel like giving up and giving in – in frenetic moments like that, we urgently need hope.

I love the way the author talks about a better hope in Hebrews 6:19 and likens it to an anchor for the soul. That means when the sands of time are shifting and sinking, we have a hope that is sure and steadfast.

Hope with a capital H gives us the encouragement we need to go on with the Lord; it enables us to fire on every cylinder for Jesus; it keeps us plodding on through deep furrows when the burdens of ministry are heavy; it helps us hang in there when life's battles are unbelievably hard. Hope is not a sedative. It is not a soporific pill that we swallow with a glass of water. It is more like a surging rush of adrenalin in the veins of the Christian. Where there is Christ, there is hope. Yes! When focused on Jesus, hope springs eternal in the human breast.

The passing of time destroys many of our fondest hopes as they slowly fade and die. As the years roll by (and the older we are, the faster they seem to go) the Christian's hope becomes much more glorious. Solomon in his wisdom said that 'the path of the righteous is like the light of dawn, which shines brighter and brighter until full day' (Proverbs 4:18). The closer we are to the Lord's appearing, the brighter that hope shines in our hearts. A new day is dawning! D L Moody testified, 'I am walking toward a bright light and the nearer I get the brighter it is.' A similar chord is struck in Jeremiah 29:11 where God came to the aid of his beleaguered servants, for whom hope appeared to have all but evaporated. He said, 'I know the plans I have for you, plans to give you hope and a future.'

That brand of hope will put a gleaming twinkle in our eyes, it will put the effervescent sparkle back into our lives, and it will add a metre to our every footstep. Why? Because we have something to live for today, and so much to look forward to in all our tomorrows. The world hopes for the best, but the Christian has the best hope. The hymn writer Jim Hill captures this inspiring theme:

There is coming a day
When no heartaches shall come,
No more clouds in the sky,
No more tears to dim the eye;
All is peace for evermore
On that happy golden shore,
What a day, glorious day, that will be.

Running scared

Paul starts the ball rolling by talking about their fear, *But we do not want you to be uninformed, brothers, about those who are asleep, that you may not grieve as others do who have no hope.*

The folk in the church in Thessalonica were extremely worried. Puzzled. Perplexed. They were going through real agony of mind. Barely a day slipped by when they did not experience deep anguish of heart. They were antsy. Restless. Fidgety. By the minute, they were getting themselves into a state of muddled anxiety. Like the proverbial string on a bow, they were uptight and riddled with doubts. It has been well said that 'doubts are the ants in the pants of faith.'

The big problem was that some of their close friends and loved ones had died and they were concerned lest those who had died would miss out at the Lord's return. What about my wife, my husband, my son, my daughter? All sorts of gargantuan questions were going through their minds: Would they be left behind? What has actually happened to them? Are they alright? Shall we see them again? Where are they now? John Stott hits the nail on the head when he writes, 'Such questions arise partly from a natural curiosity, partly from Christian concern for the dead, and partly because their death reminds us of our own mortality and undermines our security.'

That is the reason why they were so incredibly upset and I reckon, if we had been in their shoes, we would probably have felt much the same. Perfectly understandable. 'The fear of death troubles our lives like a hurricane sweeping over a serene harbour,' notes Charles Swindoll. 'And, anchored in the shallows, our little boats of faith are easily dashed against the rocks by fear's fury.'

Ignorance is not bliss

Before we get too deeply into this section, it is helpful to realise that these verses are more pastoral than theological. Paul is not writing to teach the nuances of eschatology. He is, however, going out of his way to alleviate their acute grief and give them some informed answers to their hard questions.

Donald Grey Barnhouse, pastor of historic Tenth Presbyterian Church in Philadelphia for some thirty-three years, lost his first wife to cancer. As he was driving home from her funeral with his four young children in the back seat, racked with grief, he was struggling to say some words of comfort to them. He had no idea what to say when a large moving truck passed their car, casting its huge shadow over their vehicle as it roared by. Instantly, Barnhouse, a master of illustrations, knew he had an illustration to tell his children. He said to them, 'Children, would you rather be run over by a truck or by its shadow?' The children said, 'Well, of course, Dad, we'd much rather be run over by the shadow. That can't hurt us at all.' Barnhouse replied, 'Did you know that two thousand years ago the truck of death ran over the Lord Jesus in order that only its shadow might run over us?'

You see, the foremost difficulty these sad Thessalonian believers wrestled with was that their fear was based on ignorance. And, as C H Spurgeon said, 'Half our fears are the result of ignorance.' Hence the sleepless nights and restless days. They knew a lot but they did not know all they needed to know. They knew that Jesus was coming back, but there were a lot of things that did not seem to make sense. In their state of mind, two and two did not make four. Had they mistaken what Paul taught them, or were they only a little confused about the whole event?

The fact is they eagerly wanted the Lord to come. They knew it was the climax of the ages – the great event that signalled the pinnacle of redemptive history; and they did not want to miss it! That explains why Paul says what he does in the opening phrase, *we do not want you to be uninformed.*

This is one of four key areas where Paul clearly indicates that ignorance is not bliss. The other references are: 1 Corinthians 10:1 with regard to events in the Old Testament era; Romans 11:25 in relation to the ultimate restoration of Israel; and 1 Corinthians 12:1 where he talks at length about the manifestation of spiritual gifts. Here, in verse 13, the preacher talks about death.

Death is usually the last thing we want to talk about, for it makes us squirm, feel uncomfortable, and a little awkward. We naturally recoil into a protective shell when someone brings the subject up, we much prefer to blank it out. And yet, life being what it is, we cannot walk away from it. Death tends to be an unwelcome intruder into our lives. Generally speaking, it is an uninvited guest into our homes. Death has been variously described as the king of terrors, and at the same time, it is the terror of kings. Paul himself described it as man's 'last enemy' (1 Corinthians 15:26).

Word pictures

It is intriguing to discover that the Bible uses a wide range of metaphors for death; in a remarkable way, each one shows what it is, for it demonstrates the true character of death. For example, in Proverbs 14:27 death is set before us as a snare, 'The fear of the Lord is a fountain of life, that one may turn away from the snares of death.' Another is found in Psalm 18:4 where David admitted that death is like sorrow. The shepherd king says, 'The sorrows of death have entangled me' (NIV). A third illustration is taken from Isaiah 9:2 where the great evangelical prophet sees death as a shadow. He reminds us of those who are 'living in the land of the shadow of death' (NIV). The last one is in the New Testament where we see death as a sting. Paul challenged death in 1 Corinthians 15:55 when he asked the question: 'O death, where is your sting?' And then, right here in verse 13, death is described as sleep.

It is not surprising that many cultures, from day one, have referred to death by the euphemism of sleep. It is worth noting that the word 'cemetery' is a derivation from an ancient Greek word which means 'the place of sleep'. That was how the early believers viewed it. From that perspective, it was an optimistic stance to take as it really was a synonym for a dormitory, a place where people sleep. The stillness of a corpse bears a certain resemblance to a person in slumber.

Actually, it is a phrase that occurs from time to time in the Old Testament where we read that this king or that patriarch 'rested (slept) with his fathers' (*cf.* Asa in 2 Chronicles 16:13 and Hezekiah in 2 Chronicles 32:33). The main idea in such cases is that these figures were now at rest following a lifetime of strenuous activity. On the tomb in Nyeri (near Mount Kenya) of Lord Robert Baden-Powell, founder of The Boy Scouts Association, are the words: 'I am not here, only my body is.'

Sleeping saints

Most of us appreciate that sleep is a word that promises a great deal, it reminds us that physical death is not the end. Those of us who go to bed at night expect to get up in the morning! We all know from personal experience that sleep is temporary and transient, fleeting and passing. It does not last!

When a Christian dies, it is like going to bed, for they have fallen asleep in Jesus. When they place their head on the pillow, they are waiting for the dawning of a new day, longing for the resurrection morning. After the evening of rest, there comes the morning of rejoicing. When our friends and family pass away and are taken from us, we say to them two meaningful words, 'Good night!' But, and here is the source of our great hope, when we meet again, we shall greet each other with the immortal words, 'Good morning!'

Paul gave them a brilliant illustration when he used the example of sleep to convey what happens to a Christian at the point of death. It has been said that 'Christ made sleep the name for death in the dialect of the church.' He is certainly not talking here about 'soul sleep', as some have suggested. That would be a travesty of truth, for the Christian is never more alive than when he is in the near presence of Jesus.

Coping with life after death

Paul, realist as always, now follows up his heart-warming illustration with a word of instruction. He knows that when we lose a loved one we shall sorrow, we miss them. We are crestfallen, and at times, inconsolable. We feel it deeply. Sure we do. Don Carson observes, 'The Bible everywhere assumes that those who are bereaved will grieve, and their grief is never belittled.' There is a vacant chair in the corner of the room or around the family table; there is an empty feeling in the life and the old heart throbs. Memories are precious but they can be painful, and they certainly linger.

We find ourselves in the doldrums. But, says the apostle, it is only for a short time. A wee while.

Bereavement is a most poignant human experience, and there is a fair measure of emotional shock to cope with. To lose a loved one is to lose a part of oneself. It is hard to explain and so difficult to put into words. Having lost our only son, 15-year-old Timothy, my wife and I can readily identify with the comment made by Leighton Ford, noted evangelist and mission leader, whose oldest son died in 1982 at twenty-one years of age, 'The struggle is to bring our faith and emotions together.'

When we look at the unsaved person, the man or woman who dies without knowing the spine-tingling joy of sins forgiven and a right relationship with God, they live and die without God and without hope. There is a terrible sense of finality to those words. When their curtain drops, that is it. Unbelievably sad. Tragic. Devastating. Mind you, it did not have to be that way, and it is so unnecessary. But when a Christian dies, they immediately go to be with Christ, which is immeasurably better. I read recently, 'No Christian who has ever died has regretted it!'

Staring death in the face, the pagan world stood in despair. A typical inscription on a grave reveals this fact, 'I was not. I became. I am not. I care not.' How miserable the world is about death. A poster caption read, 'The first two minutes of a man's life are the most critical.' Graffiti underneath exclaimed, 'The last two are pretty dicey as well!'

There is just no comparison, for when the Christian dies, he is absent from the body and present with the Lord

(2 Corinthians 5:6). In a sense, we do not lose a loved one, for we know where they have gone. Our grief is not a dead-end grief, for we never say a final goodbye to a fellow believer. Partings here are brief. Short-lived. There will always be another time. I often think of the words in the high-priestly prayer of the Lord Jesus for they are answered at the home-call of every believer. There, in the upper room, he interceded to his Father and said, 'Father, I desire that they also, whom you have given me, may be with me where I am, to see my glory ...' (John 17:24). That adds a new dimension to death; it puts it all in perspective, for now we see it from a slightly different angle.

4:14

How firm a foundation

Paul declares emphatically, *we believe*. It is always good to meet a man who has his feet on the ground and who knows what he believes. What does he believe? Two fundamental truths: Jesus died and the Lord has risen! This is the irreducible core of the gospel; it is what the apostles preached and what every gospel church believes. Mark Howell writes, 'That Jesus died is essential, but that he was raised from the dead is imperative.'

Here are facts that can never be altered or amended, moved or shaken. Data that is sure, stable, and solid. A glorious certainty that cannot be trashed. Cardinal truths, they are the central tenets of our faith. We say a hearty 'amen' to them. An empty cross and an empty tomb say all that needs to be said! Paul reminds them of a transforming truth: the death of Christ purchased their redemption, but the resurrection of Christ proves their redemption. 'Death is dead, love has won, Christ has conquered!' Hallelujah!

So what? Paul says, *since we believe that Jesus died and rose again, even so, through Jesus, God will bring with him those who have fallen asleep.* In other words, since that is what happened to Jesus Christ, the same will happen to those of us who know him and love him (2 Corinthians 4:14). Down here in this world, we are encouraged to walk in his footsteps (1 Peter 2:21). Jesus died on the cross, but that was not the end of the story. He rose again on the third day, on that first Easter Sunday morning. For us, we shall die, but thank God, we shall rise also. As Jesus said, 'Because I live, you also will live' (John 14:19).

Our uplift to glory is built not on a theological whimsy, but on the substitutionary death of Christ that was a perfect satisfaction to God for sin. Since Jesus fulfilled all the conditions that God laid down for the forgiveness of sin, he transformed death into sleep for us. To borrow the now famous words of Paul, at one fell swoop, the Lord effectively took the sting out of death.

Paul reminds us in 1 Corinthians 15:20 that Christ is 'the firstfruits of those who have fallen asleep.' He is the token that one day the harvest will be gathered home. What a memorable day that will be! Bodies will rise from the earth to be reunited with the soul, and we shall meet the Lord. According to 1 Peter 1:3 and Romans 8:23 we are waiting for 'the redemption of the body'. Herein lies our blessed assurance, the solid ground of our certitude. That, in a nutshell, is our hope. Bill and Gloria Gaither focus our confidence in the Lord Jesus Christ with these words:

Because he lives I can face tomorrow;
Because he lives all fear is gone;
Because I know he holds the future,
And life is worth the living
Just because he lives.

4:15

God said it, I believe it

Paul is at pains to remind them that this promise is not a figment of his fertile imagination. There is nothing illusory or dreamlike about it. He wants to reinforce his teaching to them that he is definitely not leading them up the garden path or down some blind alley. He is not pulling the wool over their eyes in order to lull them into a feeling of false security. He says, *for this we declare to you by a word from the Lord*. A divine utterance that is a direct, unabridged revelation from the living God.

John MacArthur notes, 'This is not a philosophical speculation, it is not religious mythology, and it is not some kind of fable fabricated by well-meaning people who want to make folk feel good because of their sorrow.' It is none of that. This is God's pure word, period. We take the phrase at face value: it means what it says and it says what it means! The real implication is that we can believe it, for it carries authority. One hundred percent authentic. Totally reliable. Utterly credible.

Alive or asleep

Paul then develops the argument by drawing attention to two types of people who will be most affected with the return of Christ. First, those who are alive, and second, those who are asleep.

The whole emphasis in Scripture is on the sudden return of Jesus Christ. In fact, there is nothing to stop us thinking that it may even be today. His advent is imminent and impending. The Lord is at hand as he could come back at any moment. Our redemption is nearer today than it was when we first placed our trust in him as Lord and Saviour (Luke 21:28). Jesus is standing at the threshold waiting for the final signal from the Father. It has never been so late before, the countdown to zero hour is getting lower every day. I really do believe in my heart that it is as close as that.

We may be the generation alive when Jesus breaks through the clouds. If we are, we shall not experience death. It has happened before. Yes, it has! Remember Enoch (Genesis 5:24). When his walk with the Lord ended, he left this world not through the dark tunnel of death but by walking across the golden bridge of translation. Remember Elijah (2 Kings 2:11). He is another fine example, for when his work for the Lord was done it was instant glory, the 'now you see him, now you don't' syndrome!

And when we put them both together, we can say with the gospel song, 'When labour's ended (Elijah) and the journey's done (Enoch), then he will lead me safely to my home.' Another song expressed it like this, 'O joy, O delight, should we go without dying.' Someone said, tongue in cheek, that we are not looking for the undertaker, we are looking for the up-taker! One line a hymn sums it up beautifully when it says that 'the sky, not the grave, is our goal!'

Facing the facts

There is no point in us burying our heads in the sand; we have to face reality. And the watertight fact is this: there are countless millions of God's dear people who are now absent from the body and present with the Lord. There is a vast innumerable company of choice saints who have gone on before us, and right now, they are with Christ. They have died, they have been laid to rest, and they are those, according to verse 14, who have fallen asleep in Jesus. The nagging questions are, would they:

- miss out at the second coming of Jesus?
- be downgraded to a lower category of saint?
- be no more than an eternally disembodied spirit?
- be seen as a tag-on, simply coming along for the journey?

First things first

Look another time and see the rare privilege that is theirs. Deservedly so! Yes, they will rise, says Paul, there is no question about that. But they will rise first. That is the life-changing word, *first*. They do not miss out. How could they? Why should they? They will not be left behind when Jesus comes for his own, nor will they be excluded or disadvantaged in any way. There is no remote possibility of that.

The Lord never short-changes his people. They are going to get the front seats. They will have the place of honour when the roll is called up yonder. I like to think of it like this: those who have died trusting Jesus have caught an earlier train to their final destination of glory. Today we are standing on the station platform, and who knows, we may be on the next one! That is what happens when our number is up, and our time is up.

This is what dying well, dying with dignity, is all about. It is being ready to go when the special moment arrives. As David reminds us in Psalm 23:4, we go through the valley of the shadow of death with the Shepherd alongside us. He takes us right through into the full light of his glorious presence, into a land of fadeless day. He leads us into a place where there is fulness of joy and eternal pleasures to be enjoyed. It is maybe a touch surreal when we think about it today, but it is really exciting and something to get enthused about.

Paul was absolutely right when he said in Romans 14:8 that whether we live or die, we belong to the Lord. No matter what way we look at it, if we know the Lord, we are winners every time! In light of all that Paul has been saying, let me remind you of the words of a great hymn penned by Avis M Christiansen (1895-1985):

Darkness is gathering, but hope shines within,
I know I'll see Jesus some day!
What joy when he comes to wipe out every sin,
I know I'll see Jesus some day.

I'll gladly say it again:

Sweet is the hope that is thrilling my soul,
I know I'll see Jesus some day.

I read a story of a five-year-old girl who was watching her big brother die of an incredibly painful disease. He was much older than she, and she loved him a lot. After he died and the funeral was over, she said to her mother, 'Mummy, where … where did my brother go?' Her mum took her up in her arms and said to her, 'He went to heaven to be with Jesus!' The girl said, 'O!' That was all; her mum's answer satisfied her mind, it answered her curiosity. Not long after that incident, she heard her mother having a conversation with a friend and her mum was weeping and saying, 'I've lost my son … I've lost my son … I've lost my son!' Later in the day the five-year-old went to her heartbroken mother and said, 'Mummy, is somebody lost when we know where they are?'

Now, we know the answer to that question! The answer is that no one is lost when we know where they are! That sums up in a handful of words what Paul has been saying, it crystallises his eschatology. They do not lose out in any way, and they will not miss the magical moment when Jesus comes in the air. That is the immutable promise of

Scripture and the unswerving commitment of the risen Lord to his people!

4:16-17

Signs of the times

'Maranatha' was the customary greeting in the early church (1 Corinthians 16:22). Down the street, in the market, across the fence, when God's people met one another this was what they invariably said: Maranatha! The word is Aramaic and actually means 'the Lord is coming' or 'come, O Lord'.

Two thousand years have come and gone since the Lord first made that glowing promise to his bewildered disciples in the upper room (John 14:3). So much has happened across the world since then. When we think of some key events within the last 100 years which are of cosmic significance, a lot of water has gone under the bridge: two great world wars, the establishment of the modern state of Israel, the emergence of Europe as a major player in global politics, the political clout and economic influence of China, the dollar effect in world markets (America sneezes and the rest of the world catches a cold), the fall of communism, the rise of Islam, the threat of a nuclear holocaust, globalisation, international terrorism ... and the list goes on!

Today we are well past the eleventh hour, and with the darkness deepening, time is fast running out. When we read the signs of the times, they tell us it cannot be long until Jesus returns. The prophetic clock is perfectly synchronised with God's time.

Standing on the promises

The truth that Paul emphasises in these verses could be described as the next great event on God's prophetic calendar. Lift-off for glory is number one on God's agenda for the church, the moment when millions are missing. This is the believer's ultimate trip, something to really look forward to with a purring feeling of heightened expectancy in our hearts. Is it any wonder that Paul finishes the chapter by saying that this wonderful truth should be a means of mutual encouragement to us within the global family of God.

- When the going gets tough – hang in there, Jesus is coming.

- When we feel beaten in the fight – one day we shall overcome, Jesus is coming.

- When we feel rejected and of no use to the Lord – we should not lose heart, Jesus is coming.

- When we say farewell to a loved one and life does not seem worth living – look, it will not be long until we meet up, Jesus is coming.

This is not a cop-out attitude. It is not an opt-out clause in our contract of salvation either. It is not adopting the ostrich mentality and burying our heads in the sand. It is not me saying, 'Stop the world, I must get off!' It is looking forward with a flame of hope burning in our hearts, an electrifying excitement combined with a fair bit of fervour and bated breath when we contemplate what awaits us. It is the sitting-on-the-edge-of-our-seats mindset, we are so intoxicated and inspired with this truth that we are standing on our tiptoes. Jesus Christ is coming, there is 'better on before'. The best is yet to be for we are born and bound for glory. In the words of Stuart Townend:

There is a hope that stands the test of time,
That lifts my eyes beyond the beckoning grave,
To see the matchless beauty of a day divine
When I behold his face!

According to schedule

Paul drafts out a programme, a kind of schedule (not a timetable). There are no fewer than six 'P' characteristics surrounding this wonderfully exciting event in God's unfolding purpose and plan.

- It is personal.
- It is powerful.
- It is purposeful.
- It is practical.
- It is precious.
- It is permanent.

The one returning from heaven is *the Lord himself* and that means it is personal. An angel will not be sent in his place as a last-minute substitute. No other representative from the Godhead will be despatched. No emissary will be sent from above to escort us home to heaven, Jesus is coming!

The Greek in the text is quite emphatic. There is no messing around here: Jesus is the bridegroom coming to take his bride home to heaven.

The message Jesus shared with his disciples prior to going to Calvary underlines this indestructible fact. There he told them, 'I will come again' (John 14:3). A similar message was echoed by the angels on Ascension Day as he took off from the Mount of Olives, on the east of the golden city of Jerusalem. They said, 'This Jesus, who was taken up from you into heaven, will come in the same way as you saw him go into heaven' (Acts 1:11). Nothing could be clearer. He said it himself and his word is his bond. Jesus Christ is a man of unimpeachable integrity, and there is no reason to doubt what he says.

He came and died as the Lord *of* glory; today, at the Father's right hand, he is the Lord *in* glory; when he comes in power at the end of the age, he will be the Lord *with* glory; but, at his coming in the air for his pilgrim people, he is the Lord *from* glory. We tap our feet as we hum the chorus penned by Benjamin Russell Hanby (1833-67):

'Tis the Lord! O wondrous story!
'Tis the Lord, the king of glory!
At his feet we humbly fall;
Crown him, crown him Lord of all!

Sounds from heaven

The coming of Christ is powerful. J B Phillips captures the drama, 'One word of command, one shout from the archangel, one blast from the trumpet of God and the Lord himself will come down from heaven!' When we stop and think about it, that means there are three 'sounds of welcome' intimately associated with the advent of Jesus. The first is the sound of the shout. Really, this is a military expression, and it indicates a command or an order that is given. It is as if the troops are standing at ease and the command issued is, 'Come to Attention!'

He will speak with the voice that wakes the dead. In fact, three times in the New Testament do we read of our Lord raising his voice to the level of a shout, and each time it is followed by a resurrection. The first instance is at the grave of his close friend Lazarus in John 11 when, after he spoke a few words, Lazarus emerged as large as life. There he was, standing at the doorway of the tomb. It is probably fair comment to say that if Jesus had not singled Lazarus out for special attention, he would have emptied the entire cemetery. Dennis Bennett makes the point that 'the Lord Jesus is the world's worst funeral director for he broke up every funeral he ever attended, including his own.' That says something! A track record to be proud of!

The second recorded incident was on the centre cross at Calvary when Jesus shouted in glorious victory and triumph, 'It is finished' (John 19:30). Matthew's account of this event indicates that some graves were opened and many of the saints of God arose (Matthew 27:50). The final occasion is here in verse 16. Again he will shout and an innumerable company of believers from the four corners of the earth will rise to enter into his immediate presence. Erwin Lutzer writes, 'The Lord will descend with a shout, "Get up! You've been dead long enough!" and the bodies will appear.'

I was interested to read that at the time of the millennial kingdom, it says in Psalm 47:5 that 'God has gone up with a shout, the Lord with the sound of a trumpet.' There, he goes up with a shout; but here, at phase one of his coming, he comes down with a shout!

Michael-angel

The second great mover and shaker in this 'out of this world' drama is the unexpectedly high level of involvement by the archangel Michael. He can safely be described as the chief prince of the hosts of heaven. He is number one in the angelic pecking order and it appears from reading between the lines that he has a varying range of responsibilities.

In Jude 9 he is involved in the realm of controversy in relation to the precise whereabouts of the body of Moses. In Daniel 12 and Revelation 12 he is hailed as the defender of the nation of Israel during the dark days of the period of tribulation; there we see him in a primary role of conquest. In Daniel 10 he is very much to the fore in the realm of conflict, especially as it is linked to the challenging problem of unanswered prayer.

Michael's participation is a clear signal to a watching world that three things will have happened: one, all the nefarious hordes of hell will have been roundly defeated; two, death will have lost her sting; and three, the grave will not have gained the victory. This is the singular moment in time when heaven breaks off diplomatic relations with earth. It is that one favourable moment when the blood-washed nationals of heaven are summoned home to glory.

When the trumpet of the Lord

The last notable sound in the sequence of the advent adventure is the triumph of the trump of God, the 'last trump' mentioned by Paul in 1 Corinthians 15:52. When silver trumpets sounded in the Old Testament era, it was a rallying call for the people to engage in worship, or to strike camp and walk on to some new locale, or even to go to war. The trumpets were used for all kinds of events – festivals and celebrations, convocations and judgments. They were used any time anybody wanted to assemble a crowd together to say anything to them by way of public announcements and proclamations.

I was intrigued to read in Exodus 19:16-19 that the trumpet was used to call the people out of the camp in order to meet God, a trumpet of assembly. I believe that occasion was a foreshadowing of the great event outlined here by the apostle Paul. In Zephaniah 1:16 and Zechariah 9:14 a trumpet was used as a signal of the Lord's coming to rescue his people from wicked oppression, a deliverance trumpet. On a similar note, I believe this is a mere echo of what will happen when the Lord returns to snatch us out of this present evil world. James Milton Black (1856-1938) penned the familiar words:

When the trumpet of the Lord shall sound,
And time shall be no more,

And the morning breaks, eternal, bright, and fair;
When the saved of earth shall gather
Over on the other shore,
And the roll is called up yonder,
I'll be there.

When the trumpet sounds on that great day, 'unto him will the gathering of the people be' (Genesis 49:10, NIV). Then will be held what the writer to the Hebrews referred to as 'the assembly of the firstborn who are enrolled in heaven' (12:22-23) as many sons and daughters are brought from afar and taken home to glory. This is the principal role of the one who is the captain of our salvation. Blind hymn writer Fanny Crosby (1820-1915) expressed it well:

What a gathering, what a gathering,
What a gathering of the ransomed
In the summer land of love,
What a gathering, what a gathering,
Of the ransomed in that happy home above.

Take heart! When we think of the noise associated with this rather auspicious and grand occasion, there is no way we shall ever sleep through it!

Raison d'être

Sometimes we ask the fairly obvious question: Why is Jesus coming back? It is purposeful, for here is the reason behind it: he is coming for you and me. First, the dead, and then, the living. This is a capital truth that oozes words of bright encouragement. It reiterates the judicious belief that those who have gone on before us are not treated as second-class citizens in the kingdom of God. In no sense will they lag behind the rest of us who are alive and kicking when the Lord returns.

It also affirms our eternal position in Christ, for Paul refers to the *dead in Christ*. A lovely phrase. The bottom line is this: if we are in Christ, we are always in Christ, whether alive or dead! 'And,' as John MacArthur says, 'when you die and that body goes into the grave, that body reposes in Christ. That belongs exclusively to him. That is his personal and eternal possession and he will reclaim it from its decomposed dust.' This is the heartbeat of Paul's teaching at the end of Romans 8 where he reminds us that nothing and no one can separate us from the love of God in Christ Jesus. We are glued to him with an unbreakable bond. Union with Christ is the label that theologians give to it. Because of grace, we are hermetically sealed and we routinely find our focus in him.

- we live in Christ
- we die in Christ
- we are dead in Christ
- we stay in Christ
- we shall live again in Christ

Caught up!

What is the Lord coming back to do? At the risk of sounding simplistic, we shall be transported supernaturally into a new world. He is returning to snatch the saints away and he will do it with an awesome use of irresistible force: snatched from the clutches of Satan, snatched from the fallen world, snatched from the serious limitations of the flesh, snatched from the jaws of death, snatched from the confines of the grave, and snatched away from the coming wrath of God.

The one who, in a moment of time, plucked us as brands from the burning will, in that final day, pluck us out of this present evil world. When he returns, he will claim us for himself, and as if that is not enough, he will relocate us by moving us into a new place for our eternal habitation, a place he is preparing for us right now, the city of the living God.

This is all entailed in the phrase employed by John in Revelation 20:5 when he speaks of the first resurrection. It is interesting to note that there are three phases to this particular activity, each of which corresponds to the Jewish harvest. They spoke of the time when the firstfruits were reaped and presented to the Lord Jehovah; a while later, the harvest was gathered home; and that was followed by the picking up of the gleanings. A fuller account is detailed in God's calendar of redemption in Leviticus 23:9-14.

In relation to our Lord's programme, this would remind us of the firstfruits being gathered in at his resurrection on that first Easter Sunday morning, the harvest will ultimately take place as and when the trumpet sounds, and the gleanings will be collected at various times during the period of seven years tribulation.

In the twinkling of an eye

His coming is practical, for in that day 'we shall all be changed' (1 Corinthians 15:51). It probably appeals to my warped sense of humour, but I cannot help but think that this is an excellent verse to hang on the wall of a church crèche where 'we shall not all sleep, but we shall all be changed!'

It will transpire in a moment; in Paul's words, in the 'twinkling of an eye' (1 Corinthians 15:52). The question is: How long does it take for your eye to twinkle? Kwesi, a consultant ophthalmologist friend, shared with me that it is approximately one-tenth to one-twentieth of a second! It will be just as fast as that, quicker than the drop of a hat or the flick of a switch. Talk about split-second speed, Jesus does not drag his heels.

And when it occurs, see what he is going to do. He will give us all a brand new body, and at the same time, kit us out for heaven. We shall be fitted for glory in clothing with God's designer label attached. The decay, disease, and weaknesses that plague and ravage our body now will be stripped away. The things that tear and wear us down will no longer have a grip on us.

This body of humiliation will become a body of glorification (Philippians 3:21), this mortal frame will put on immortality, and this body which is presently corruptible will put on incorruption (1 Corinthians 15:53). In a flash, we shall be like the Lord Jesus himself. Some words penned by Horatius Bonar (1808-89) are so apt at this point:

'Twas sown in weakness here;
'Twill then be raised in power;
That which was sown an earthly seed
Shall rise a heav'nly flower.

This is where the words of John the beloved apostle come into sharp focus, for he says in his first epistle, 'We know that, when he appears, we shall be like him for we shall see him as he is' (3:2). When Jesus returns, he will upgrade all his people to the status of Christlikeness in their own body. An irreversible act. The extraordinary work of sanctification initiated at the point of our conversion will then be complete. The astoundingly good work he began within our hearts when we handed over our lives to him will then be finished (Philippians 1:6).

We'll understand it better

The coming of the Lord Jesus is exceedingly precious for we shall not only be like him, we shall be with him and that for all eternity. The meeting in the air will be the best, biggest, and brightest meeting we shall ever be in. No wonder it is in the air, for there is not a stadium on earth that could contain the goodly crowd.

Satan is labelled 'the prince of the power of the air' (Ephesians 2:2), but on that day the air will not be his domain, it will belong to the believer. We shall be on cloud nine, a seventh-heaven experience: as pleased as Punch, and totally enamoured with Jesus as the centre of attraction. Death is the great separator but Jesus Christ at his advent is the great reconciler.

It holds the mouth-watering prospect of a happy and joyful reunion as we link up with those who have preceded us. It will be the most impressive family reunion in history. I have no doubts at all that we shall recognise our loved ones in heaven, and together we shall worship the King in his impeccable beauty. The Bible does not reveal all the details of this reunion; it is strangely silent on the subject. We are left to read between the lines, as it were. When Jesus raised the widow's son from the dead, we read in Luke 7:15 that he tenderly 'gave him back to his mother' (NIV). This seems to suggest that our Lord will have the felicitous role of reuniting broken families and friendships. On snow-capped Hermon, the Mount of Transfiguration, the three disciples knew and recognised Moses and Elijah (Matthew 17:1-5). They did not have to be introduced and this appears to indicate that we shall know our loved ones in heaven.

There are many things in life that we do not fully understand, but then we shall know and they will all make sense (John 13:7). Many questions today go unanswered, but over there all will be made plain. 'We'll understand it better by and by.' Our dilemma is that so long as we are citizens on earth, we see through tinted glass, but then it will be face to face (1 Corinthians 13:12). The hymn writer Carrie Ellis Breck (1855-1934) picked up that theme when she wrote:

Face to face with Christ, my Saviour,
Face to face – what will it be,

When with rapture I behold him,
Jesus Christ who died for me?

In this life we only see the underside of the tapestry with coloured threads hanging all over the place, and at times it does not look particularly good. It is difficult to recognise the pattern when lying face down on the carpet! Too close for comfort. Standing on heaven's golden shore, however, we shall fully appreciate the words of Anne Ross Cousin:

I'll bless the hand that guided,
I'll bless the heart that planned,
When throned where glory dwelleth
In Immanuel's land.

Over there Romans 8:28 will become a fabulously sweet reality. You see, death shortens our way to heaven, but grace sweetens our way to heaven. The poem penned by Benjamin Malachi Franklin (1882-1965) of Mississippi puts into words the deep-down sentiments of many of our hearts:

Not till the loom is silent
And the shuttles cease to fly,
Will God unroll the canvas
And explain the reason why,
The dark threads are as needful
In the weaver's skilful hand,
As the threads of gold and silver
In the pattern he has planned.

It is worth noting that the word *meet* carries the idea of meeting a royal person or an important person. That says it all, for we could not encounter anyone more important than our Lord Jesus Christ. And we certainly could not ever hope to rendezvous with anyone of such regal splendour as the one who is acknowledged as King of kings, Prince of princes, and Lord of lords. Moments with majesty.

On and on, and on

How long will it last? A day, a week, a month, a year? No! Thank God, it is permanent. It is *forever with the Lord*. Eternal. Perpetual. Bliss unending. Pleasures for evermore (Psalm 16:11). For us, it will have an entry point, but there is no exit, for we are there to stay! I love the words of the hymn penned by James Montgomery (1771-1854), a former Sheffield newspaper editor:

> *'Forever with the Lord!'*
> *Amen, so let it be!*
> *Life from the dead is in that word,*
> *'Tis immortality.*
> *Here in the body pent,*
> *Absent from him I roam,*
> *Yet nightly pitch my moving tent*
> *A day's march nearer home.*
>
> *So when my latest breath*
> *Shall rend the veil in twain,*

By death I shall escape from death,
And life eternal gain.
That resurrection-word,
That shout of victory:
Once more, 'Forever with the Lord!'
Amen, so let it be!

The great goal of redemption is not just to rescue us from sin and judgment, but to relate us to Christ. We shall enjoy face-to-face contact with the Lover of our souls, and that for ever. An exciting prospect which sets the pulse racing and the heart beating faster. The years that must pass, before it all breaks in upon us, will seem like seconds once the joy of it has burst upon us.

- What a consummation!
- What communion!
- What a Christ!

4:18

Cheer up ... Jesus is coming!

Paul said, *Therefore encourage one another with these words.* If this great truth does not encourage us, I do not know what else will. Paul does not say that these monumental truths should prompt us to set dates, or sell our possessions, or watch for Christ's return from the highest mountain. Nor does he suggest that we should go our merry way without paying any further regard to these future events. When it comes to the Lord's return, we are on the welcoming committee, not the organising committee.

God wants us to take this knowledge and use it to cheer and comfort one another. When we grieve, we need to be encouraged with these truths, so that our sorrow is permeated with hope, not despair. We find enormous strength in the fact that one day our Lord will call us home to be with himself: strength even when we cannot understand why bad things happen to good people; strength when we wonder if our evangelistic efforts are worthwhile; strength when we become tired and weary of struggling against temptation; strength when we feel crushed with all the hassles and hurts of this life.

When we think of the return of the Lord Jesus, there is:

- a sound to hear
- a sight to see
- a miracle to feel
- a meeting to enjoy
- a comfort to experience

We know the Lord is coming, but we do not know when. Therefore, we pull out all the stops and walk close with the Lord. We stay close to Jesus. Will Christ's return be an embarrassing intrusion or a glorious climax to life for us? When we think seriously about the second coming of Jesus, does that thought bring peace and excitement to our hearts, or does it foster frustration and uneasiness?

At any moment

A tourist was exploring the sites of Lake Como in northern Italy and came to a beautiful castle. Feeling brave, he pushed open the ornamental iron gate and ventured inside. To his delight, everything was elegantly A-1. Flowers were blooming in a rainbow of extravagant colour. The shrubbery was luxuriously green and magnificently manicured to precision.

Over to the side, the man noticed a gardener on his hands and knees clipping nearly every blade of grass. He asked, 'May I walk around and have a look at the gardens?' The gardener replied, 'Sure, you're welcome. Come right in. I'm glad to have a guest.'

The visitor began to tour the expansive grounds and asked the gardener, 'Is the owner here today?'

The gardener replied, 'No, I'm afraid not. He's away.'

'When was the last time you saw him?' he asked.

'About twelve years ago,' said the gardener.

'Twelve years? You mean, this idyllic place has been empty for twelve years?' exclaimed the tourist.

'Yes,' said the unruffled gardener.

The inquisitive tourist asked, 'Who tells you what to do?'

The gardener explained that the owner had an agent in Milan.

'Do you ever see him?' enquired the tourist.

Still clipping, pruning, and trimming, the gardener answered, 'Never. He just sends instructions.'

The tourist could not believe his ears. 'But everything is so pristinely beautiful. It is perfect. It looks like you're expecting him tomorrow.'

The gardener replied, 'Today, sir. I expect him to come at any time. Perhaps today!'

It may be today

Each day is one day nearer. Each step is one step closer. On that expectant note, maybe we need to cry out with John who, when exiled on the craggy Isle of Patmos, said, 'Amen. Come, Lord Jesus!' (Revelation 22:20). The words penned by Beatrice Bush Bixler (1916-2013) resonate with my heart:

The Christ I love is coming soon,
It may be morning, night, or noon.
My lamps are lit, I'll watch and pray.
It may be today, it may be today.

Mark #5

A church where grace is experienced

A *Mother Goose & Grimm* comic strip – dated 4 September 1997 – featured this question: 'What is the difference between ignorance and apathy?' The answer: 'I don't know and I don't care!' That is the way a lot of people feel about the return of Jesus Christ, they do not know and they do not really care. Yet the Bible keeps repeating the theme over and over again. Sadly, some folk have switched off. They have grown used to it in the same way that people become accustomed to the familiar Westminster chimes of a grandfather clock in their lounge.

Making the connection

Every time Jesus and Paul talked about the future, they connected it to the present. Bible prophecy was never meant to be an end in itself. The whole purpose of prophetic truth is not to tickle our ears as we engage in hours of mindless speculation; it is more like a catalyst to spur us on. It is the great motivator. The end times should cause us to reshuffle our priorities in the present times, helping us set our personal agenda so that we live out a radical gospel before needy men and women.

The nearness of the Lord's return should compel us to share the gospel more urgently, it should drive us to serve him more faithfully, and it should be the incentive we need to give ourselves to others more freely. This high-powered truth is specifically designed to light a fire under our lives, to fan the flame of godly living in our hearts.

Left behind

The return of Jesus will have a profound effect upon those who are left behind. For the Christian, as we saw in the previous chapter, it is great, for a new day is dawning. That noble truth is what prompted the prince of Scottish hymn writers, Horatius Bonar, to sing:

I see the last dark bloody sunset,
I see the dread Avenger's form,
I see the Armageddon's onset,
But I shall be above the storm.

For the sinner, it is not quite so good, for the night is falling and the darkness is deepening. To one, the future is sheeny bright and inspiring; to the other, the future is bleak and eerily ominous. The long night-time of Satan's dominion will soon give way to the sunup of Christ's coming for his own. The Puritan preacher, Thomas Watson, helpfully comments, 'Eternity to the godly is a day that has no sunset; eternity to the wicked is a night that has no sunrise.'

It may help if we looked at it like this: phase one of the advent programme is when Jesus comes in the air for his people (4:16); phase two is when the Lord comes to the earth with his people (Revelation 19:11-16). Stage one is the *parousia*; stage two is the *epiphania* from which we get our English word, epiphany. Primarily, it speaks of the revelation, the unveiling, of Christ.

In these verses, Paul draws back the curtain and shows us what happens in between the two stages of the Lord's return. Paul envisages an event taking place which he calls *the day of the Lord*, a day of devastation, destruction, doom, and damnation. Paul informs us in this earth-moving section of this climactic, cataclysmic day, soon to come in human history. The bottom line is this: there is a woefully serious crisis facing the sinner.

5:1

History is his story

Paul begins by saying, *Now … brothers*. That is a giveaway phrase, it is a clear indication that he is about to introduce a brand new subject, a classic telltale sign that he is moving on to new ground which he has not covered before. He is turning a corner, as he wants to look at coming events from a fresh perspective; he wants to view things from a different direction.

In his next breath, Paul refers to *the times and the seasons*, an interesting phrase that only appears three times in Scripture in Daniel 2:21, Acts 1:7, and here. When our Lord used the term in Acts 1 it was in reference to Israel, not to the church of Jesus Christ. It speaks about the coming kingdom. That is why Paul says, *concerning the times and the seasons ... you have no need to have anything written to you*. It is worth pointing out that two different Greek words are used, *chronos* 'times' and *kairos* 'seasons', two kinds of time. John Stott reminds us that 'usually *chronos* means a period of time and *kairos* a point of time, a crisis or opportunity.' If we take a moment and separate the two words, *chronos* is the word from which we derive our English word 'chronology', meaning clock time or calendar time. The other word, *kairos*, means seasons, epochs, or events. It looks at time, not from the specific viewpoint of a day and an hour; rather, it views time from the perspective of an event, an epoch, something significant that has happened.

In this context, the folk in the church in Thessalonica are curious about events that relate to the end of the world and they are fascinated and want to know more about the epochs that shape and mark the end of time. The fact is, some things they definitely need to know, some of the finer details in the small print they do not need to know, and some things they know already! Hence the wisdom of Warren Wiersbe's comment that 'the second coming of Christ is not a toy to play with, but a tool to build with.'

5:2-3

Blind date

Paul goes on the offensive when he says, *for you yourselves are fully aware*. It is fascinating to discover that the phrase *fully aware* comes from the Greek word *akribos* meaning 'you know exactly'. It is a word that emerges out of painstaking research whereby someone is able to arrive at a logical conclusion.

Paul says, 'Look, you guys know precisely what I am talking about, you know perfectly well what I mean when I say what I do; you know with a high degree of accuracy that this great event is something which is totally unexpected – I have told you that already!' It sounds as though Paul is getting fairly hot under the collar with those individuals who had nothing better to do with their time other than speculate about the future.

It seems to me that he lectured them like this: 'You know that nobody knows the date and therefore you cannot know it either!' God has chosen in his sovereign wisdom to leave us in the dark about the date. Even his Son, the Lord Jesus, does not know when it is! Why? So that every generation would live with the reality that it may happen in their lifetime. Therefore, it is not what we say we do not know that should concern us; it is what we do know already that should really bother us!

All things apocalyptic

Having cleared the air, the veteran Paul goes on to talk about the *day of the Lord* and its special significance to the end-time sequence of events. This is a most intriguing phrase as it pops up all over the place, especially in the prophetic section of the Old Testament. We read about it in half a dozen minor prophets – Joel, Amos, Obadiah, Zephaniah, Zechariah, and Malachi; and in the trio of major prophets – Isaiah, Jeremiah, and Ezekiel. In virtually every instance it is an incredibly negative picture that is painted. The focus is on judgment and anger, desolation and havoc being mercilessly wreaked on this earth. It is a vigorous attempt to bring the average citizen low; it is all about driving people to their knees.

Six times it is referred to as a day of doom and four times it is spoken of as a day of vengeance. On the day of Pentecost, Peter made more than a passing reference to it in his sermon (Acts 2:14-36), and later on, he wrote about it in his second epistle (2 Peter 3:10). It is also mentioned in the gospels of Matthew and Luke, and again, John in Revelation covers a lot of ground. Whatever the New Testament writers understood about the day of the Lord, they gleaned their info from the Old Testament prophets. It is, therefore, a biblical term, a solidly Scriptural expression.

There are many 'days' mentioned in the Bible:

- 'the days of Jesus' life on earth' – the time lapse from Bethlehem to Calvary (Hebrews 5:7)

- 'the day of salvation' – this present age when God's grace is drawing people to himself (2 Corinthians 6:2)

- 'the day of Christ' – the coming millennium when Jesus will rule and reign on earth (Philippians 1:6)

- 'the day of God' – a future eternity (2 Peter 3:12)

Satan's reign of terror

When we speak about the day of the Lord, we are talking about a period of severe trial on earth which falls in between the two stages of the advent of Jesus Christ. This is referred to as a time of 'great tribulation' in Matthew 24:21 and Revelation 7:14. It is designed to last seven years, and it should never be seen as a period only spanning twenty-four hours. It is much too intense and far-reaching for it to be crammed into a single day! And that is the issue Paul is addressing here in a thumbnail sketch.

Jeremiah describes it as 'the time of Jacob's trouble' (30:7). The evangelical prophet, Isaiah, sees it as 'the day of vengeance of our God' (61:2). John later refers to it in Revelation as 'the day of wrath of the Lamb' (6:16-17). Joel portrays it as a 'great' and 'dreadful' day (2:11). Reading between the lines, this will be a time slot of frightening, spine-chilling, blood-curdling events. It is a day of unprecedented happenings, many of them outlined in the Olivet Discourse of Matthew 24. Much of what will happen is also detailed in the centre section of Revelation, chapters 6 through 19. Scary stuff. Enough to make the hair stand up on the back of your neck. Here is the fate of Planet Earth in the day when Jesus Christ rises to shake the nations.

Predicting the unpredictable

The out-of-the-blue suddenness of such a moment is presented with vivid clarity, for it will come *like a thief in the night*. We need to show a touch of realism at this point. The triple truth of the matter is:

- No one knows when a thief is coming.
- No one really expects a thief to come.
- No one sits up and waits for a thief to come.

He just comes! Unannounced. Unscheduled. Unexpected. No advance warning. No heads-up. And as far as the ungodly are concerned, he will take everything from them. It is not the norm for a burglar to send a you-have-been-warned postcard to his potential victim. Even an Irish thief does not leave a calling card!

A Texan called into Sam's Club one afternoon. In his keenness to pick up his latest piece of gadgetry, he suffered a senior moment and left his car keys in the ignition. Ten minutes later when he came out of the store, the car was gone. He contacted the police department and they whisked him home. On the journey he did nothing but berate human nature saying how bad people really were.

Next morning when he opened the curtains he could hardly believe his eyes. His pride-and-joy Cadillac was sitting outside, gleamingly immaculate, valeted inside and out. When he opened the door, he found a note which read, 'Dear Sir, I'm sorry for taking your car. It was a dire emergency, please accept my apology. I have filled your tank with gas and have enclosed two complimentary tickets for the Dallas Cowboys.'

The Texan could not believe his luck, he was overwhelmed with the apparent kindness and thoughtfulness of the person who had temporarily borrowed his vehicle. That evening he and his wife went to the ball game. Wonderful!

However, upon returning home, when they walked in through their front door they very quickly realised the place had been ransacked. All their stuff was gone, they had been cleaned out. You see, the thief also had their house key!

People are unprepared. In all honesty, they never really expect it to take place in the first instance. It happens to the man three doors down the road, not them! They feel safe living in a cotton-wool cocoon in cloud cuckoo land. When it happens, as it will, they are caught on the hop, with an omelette on their face.

The schedule is unmistakably clear: when the trumpet sounds, the Lord comes in the air, and the Christians are immediately translated to glory. At that point the Holy Spirit is removed and the 'man of lawlessness' or the Antichrist, as he is better known, is revealed (2 Thessalonians 2:3). The whole world is taken by surprise as a cynical populace is caught napping. Sound asleep! Basically, man falls down on two counts:

- He failed to hear the word of God.
- He failed to heed decisive warnings from God.

Not unlike an event in Boston in 1919 … . In 2004 the Boston Public Library opened a new exhibit to commemorate the 85th anniversary of a strange event, the Great Molasses Flood, that killed 21 people and injured 150. On 15 January 1919 an enormous steel vat, containing 2.3 million gallons of molten molasses, burst. Hot sticky waves of syrup thirty-feet tall destroyed buildings, crushed freight cars, wagons, automobiles, and drowned people. One author called it the 'Dark Tide'. The enormous tank had been poorly designed. Company officials reacted to the constant leaks by repainting the tank to match the leaking molasses. Out of sight, out of mind!

Management knew the molasses vat was dangerous, but did not do anything about it. Their only contribution was to give the vat the appearance of normality. The lesson is: what we ignore today may drown someone tomorrow. When it comes to the end times and tomorrow's world, the man is a fool who pretends nothing is wrong by painting over the seeping cracks!

Spiritual hallucination

The unbelievable seriousness of the day of the Lord is intimated when the apostle describes it as a time of delusion for they will be saying *peace and security* when, in reality, there is none. It is conspicuous by its absence. Anything there is will be transitory in nature and will not last for long.

It is also hailed as a time of menacing darkness. Morally and spiritually, it is an era when the heart of man is as black as coal. In the natural world there will be certain phenomena as hinted in Joel 2:10 that will cause a measure of darkness as the sun, moon, and stars withdraw their shining. The Lord himself said, 'For then there will be great tribulation, such as has not been from the beginning of the world until now, no, and never will be' (Matthew 24:21). So this day is unexpected and unmitigated.

It is a time of turbulent chaos and intercontinental destruction. Like a surfer being forced under by too large a wave, this is wipeout. A repeat of the Holocaust, only this time it will be so much worse that it does not bear thinking about. As the pace of events unfolds at fever pitch, all will reach a climax at Armageddon, often referred to as World War 3. The conflict of the ages will zoom in on the devastating consequences of man's pugnacious decision to ignore the pleadings of God's Spirit to trust his Son.

In the labour ward

The primary signs of the Lord's coming, Paul tells us, are like *labour pains come upon a pregnant woman*. An interesting metaphor and one that is fairly common in Jewish apocalyptic literature. At first, the pains are not intense at all. My female sources tell me they are more uncomfortable than painful. They are bearable. A woman may feel one, and then not feel another for fifteen or twenty minutes or more. But as the moment of birth approaches, the pain gets more acute and the pains get closer together. There comes a point where the woman has to make a dash for the maternity wing of the local hospital! The birth of a child cannot be delayed.

- The pain grows.
- The intensity grows.
- The frequency grows.
- And then … a child is born.

Times will be frightfully bad, but to add fuel to the raging fire they will escalate out of hand so rapidly. The world and global affairs will appear to be recklessly out of control, but God's finger remains on the button. It is a time of tumultuous judgment, from an angry God, on the nations of the world.

However, after this, and after the purging of the nation of Israel, there will be born the age of the kingdom. Yes, there will be weeping and pain for a handful of years. Then Christ will come in phase two of his advent programme; and after a long troublesome night of seven years, joy will come in the morning. There are drearily dark days ahead for this world, but for the sinner, the worst is yet to come.

5:4-5

Sheep and goats

The difference between the groups of people Paul is talking about is crystal clear from the terms he employs. It is true in every sense to say that there are only two kinds of people in the world, those who know the Lord and those who do not. Saints and sinners, and there is no one else!

It is a classic them-and-us situation. Paul speaks of the believers as *you*, he refers to the unbelievers as *those*. The contrast is patently obvious when Paul says, we are *children of light* and they are *in darkness*. In a similar vein, he says, we are *children of the day* and *not of the night or of the darkness*.

A catchy title over these few verses might read something like this, night people versus day people! See what Paul says about each of them. Night people are associated with darkness, sleep, and drunkenness; day people are associated with light, alertness, and soberness. There is a world of difference in the here and now, but there is also a huge difference in the there and then. In the grand scheme of things, we are worlds apart!

This idea comes out very powerfully in verse 9 where Paul says, *For God has not destined us for wrath, but to obtain salvation through our Lord Jesus Christ*. In other words, the Christian will never experience wrath, as we have been chosen by grace to receive the free gift of salvation. Believers will never know wrath, as we have been appointed to know Jesus. That takes us right back to 1:4 and the durable doctrine of election, the only way to escape the coming judgment. In that sense, gospel people are unique!

Darkness and light

So far as the apostle is concerned, there is no hazy blur in his mind when it comes to the ultimate destiny of those who know the Lord. By the same token, there is no confusion in his thinking as to the eventual destiny of those who do not know the Lord. For one, it will be eternal light, a place where God's face is seen; for the other, it spells everlasting darkness, a place where God's face is hidden.

It follows, therefore, because of who we are and what we are, that we are meant to be different! Here is a resoundingly stirring challenge to the people of God. Paul pulls no punches as he tells it like it is. He is straight to the point, he goes for the jugular every time when he says, 'Get a wiggle on!' Up and doing!

The question is: How can we reach such a state of preparedness? We do not want to be caught trafficking in sin when our Saviour breaks through the clouds and comes to deliver us. We need to keep our house in order in anticipation of his imminent return. We also need to get the word out to the world that no one need experience the dreadfully awful horrors of the day of the Lord.

Paul puts his head on the block when he says to the believer: do not be indifferent today because tomorrow is secure. To the non-Christian, there is an equally forthright, no-holds-barred message: do not be fooled because today seems calm, there is a storm brewing on the horizon.

5:6

Sleep walkers

Be awake! The North Carolinian preacher, Vance Havner, said, 'This is a day of anarchy in the world, apostasy in the professing church, and apathy in the true church.' We are not meant to be spiritual Rip Van Winkles. There is no room for apathy, laziness, or complacency in God's kingdom of light. We need to snap out of our comatose lethargy and be liberated from a couldn't-care-less attitude. This is not the time for gospel people to rest on their laurels.

In today's speak, Paul is saying, do not begin to dream like the world around you is dreaming, do not fall into the trap of living in a fantasy world of make-believe. Our purpose for living in the third millennium is not to accumulate massive wealth or make a big name for ourselves; our real reason for living is to use our abilities to the full in the centre of the will of God. We need to get serious and stay in the orbit of God's plan for our lives. And be real. And relevant. To put it simply, if we belong to the day, our behaviour must be daytime behaviour. Let's not sleep or even yawn our way through this life. As gospel people, we stop living in silk pyjamas. Stay awake!

On the qui vive

Be alert. Actually, we should be living our lives in a constant state of red alert. Hawk-eyed. Eagle-eyed. Vigilant. On the lookout. Our eyes should be open wide so that we lead a life that is balanced. The thought here is of someone whose feathers are not easily ruffled, who has a calm outlook on life. It is the kind of person who hears tragic news but he does not lose heart, someone who experiences difficulties but does not give up, for he knows his future is secure in God's hands. Unflappable. Nonchalant.

The world can be roughly divided into three groups of people: the few who make things happen, the many who watch things happen, and the vast majority who have no idea what in the world is happening. Paul warns us in this verse not to be categorised by the ignorance of the masses, but to always be on our toes.

5:7

The beer factor

The contrast is glaringly obvious when we look at the unconverted person as Paul describes him, for they are said to be like drunken men whiling the hours away in a stupor. He writes, *For those who sleep, sleep at night, and those who get drunk, are drunk at night.* Such folk are enmeshed in a fool's false paradise, oblivious to the harsh realities of what lies before them. They keep their lives on track by using the drugs that the world provides. Their lack of sobriety is self-inflicted. Self-induced. They have no one else to blame but themselves. If they slouch around with a befuddled mind that cannot think clearly, that is their problem. Intoxication and inebriation with the devil's demon of alcohol will do all sorts of wild and weird things to the system.

Not convinced? Take a walk downtown any weekend and look at the poor souls coming out of the pubs, bars, and clubs, the worse for wear! These folk batten down the hatches, they put a lid on life, and their problems are blanked out; the trouble is, it does not last! They are not looking for, nor are they alert to the things of God. Basically, they are so wrapped up in themselves, they are garishly overdressed. Their hedonistic pursuit of pleasure is such that they flatly reject anything that remotely smacks of God.

5:8

Battle ready

Be armoured! Paul writes, *But since we belong to the day, let us be sober, having put on the breastplate of faith and love, and for a helmet the hope of salvation.*

- Wake up!
- Get up!
- Clean up!
- Dress up!

The picture is of a soldier on duty. The coat of armour provided is designed to protect and preserve us. It covers our vital organs, and it means we are not needlessly exposed to the enemy. With a single stroke of his pen, Paul effectively eliminates the vulnerability of the sentry on guard duty. He will be all right; he will be fine so long as he is wearing the armour! George Duffield (1818-88) wrote the familiar hymn in which he encourages us to:

Stand up, stand up for Jesus!
Stand in his strength alone:
The arm of flesh will fail you;
Ye dare not trust your own.
Put on the gospel armour,
Each piece put on with prayer;
Where duty calls, or danger,
Be never wanting there.

The breastplate could be made from a variety of metals or materials such as chain mail, or gold, or heavy cloth, or iron, or leather. At the end of the day, the material did not really matter; what counted more than anything else was the high level of protection it offered to the soldier. In our day, it is comparable to a bulletproof vest.

The parallel to the helmet in today's world is a motorcycle helmet, something that protects the head from potentially fatal blows. It is interesting that many motorcyclists in America today still reject the idea of wearing a helmet, wanting to feel the wind in their hair and be better attuned to their environment. However exhilarating that may be, it is still high risk when it comes to head injuries.

Paul was not the first to employ such excellent imagery for he borrowed this absorbing concept from Isaiah 59:17. He describes this armour in Romans 13:12 as 'the armour of light'. Faith and love are like a breastplate to cover the heart, faith toward God and a love for the people of God. Hope is a helmet that protects the mind. In two lines of text, we have faith and love and hope, a triad of supreme Christian qualities; three lofty virtues we expect to find in anyone who is walking in the light.

Facing down the enemy

Faith, hope, and love can be effectively used as three great defences when we meet temptation. Faith is a bulwark against the devious tactics of the enemy. In what sense is that true in our lives? Put it like this: sin is a result of distrusting God. To be honest, I cannot spell it out any clearer than that! The Lord is someone who is eminently worthy and deserving of our trust.

For example, we can trust the Lord's person, for he will be consistent with his attributes, he will never deviate from his character, he has perfect integrity. We can trust his power, for nothing is too difficult for him, nothing is too hard for him, nothing overwhelms him, and no one gets the better of him! We can trust his promise, for his word is his bond; if he says something, he will do it; if he promises something, he will keep it. We can trust his plan, for the Lord reigns, he is sovereign and in total control of all that happens in our lives. God does what he does because he is who he is!

The ramifications of this are incredible, if we believe it! When temptation strikes at our weakest point, we have nothing to fear; there is no need for us to fall into the trap set by the enemy, for if we do, we are casting a dark cloud of aspersion on the credibility of God. To nail it down, it means that when we buckle and cave in under pressure and start to worry about the future then we are really saying, 'Lord, we know you said you are in charge, and we know you said this problem was no big deal to you, and we know you said you could handle it, and we know you are working to a plan, we just do not believe it at this moment in time!' No doubt about it, we are the losers if we end up going into that cul-de-sac; however, we are on the winning side if we accept that God knows what is best for every one of us.

A soft side, not a soft touch

Faith acts as a breastplate. That is the hard side! Any military history student will tell you that a Roman shield also had a soft side! Underneath that hard armour was soft cloth to warm the body. And that, says Paul, is love! This is the other side of the plate, as it were. 'The outer surface shines with faith and the inner surface is lined with love,' writes John MacArthur.

All sin in our lives reflects a failure to love the Lord in a way that we should. When we think about love, we are thinking about that which is the prime object of our affection and adoration. Whoever is the supreme focus of our love is going to control what we do, what we say, and what we think. In effect, they are going to become our god! The Lord Jesus is the only one who deserves to occupy that unique place in our hearts. So when we sin and when we succumb to temptation, we are really saying that the Lord is not Number One in our thinking, he has been sidelined to just another figure in our lives. He has been elbowed out to make room for another!

See what Paul is driving at: the hard side of our breastplate, that resilient, resistant strength is that we believe God; the soft side is that we love the Lord. And when the two of them are interwoven and fully operational, we become impregnable!

Helmet of hope

A quote from Rubem Alves appeared on Facebook, where he said, 'Hope is hearing the melody of the future. Faith is to dance to it.' Paul moves on to talk about the helmet of hope! In Ephesians 6:17 it was 'the helmet of salvation'. Here it is the *hope of salvation as a helmet* (NIV). The subtle difference between the two renderings is the inclusion of the word 'hope'. That begs the question: What is our hope? It is the inescapable fact that one day Jesus Christ is returning for his people. Paul refers here to the future aspect of our salvation. We shall protect ourselves against the cruel ravages of temptation when we realise what we are going to become in the glory!

John MacArthur encapsulates all that Paul is sharing with us in this verse, when he writes, 'When faith is weak, love is cold; when love is cold, hope is lost. When faith is strong, love is zealous; when love is zealous, hope is firm.' That is what marks out a real, card-carrying Christian from the cynical Joe Blow strolling around the shopping mall.

The genuine believer with an authentic lifestyle is someone characterised by faith, love, and hope; this is his battledress, and at the same time, it is his defence against the inexorable onslaught of the deeds of darkness. True then – no less true today: light and darkness are at opposite ends of the spectrum. Poles apart. If we know Jesus as Lord and Saviour, we are sons of the light and sons of the day; we are different from other people, we are meant to be, and that is the way God intended it should be.

5:9-10

The genius of grace

So far, Paul has linked how we should behave to who we are: children of the day, and sons of the light. Now he goes on to base who we are on who God is and on what he has done for us, for we read, *For God has not destined us for wrath, but to obtain salvation through our Lord Jesus Christ, who died for us so that whether we are awake or asleep we might live with him*. Paul makes two defining statements in this duo of verses. In verse 9 he tells us quite specifically what God did not do, and in verse 10 he spells out the implications of what Jesus Christ has done!

It is enormously helpful to join the two declarations together. First, from a more positive angle, God appointed us to receive the gift of salvation; second, the Lord Jesus died for us so that we might live eternally in him. Our ultimate salvation, therefore, depends on the ripening of God's purpose, and our future life rests solely on the death of Jesus. Our hope of salvation (which Paul referred to in verse 8) is well founded for it stands firmly on the solid rock of God's sovereign will and Christ's atoning death. It is not resting on the shifting sands of our own performance or roller-coaster feelings. Sometimes we are like a yo-yo, up and down! Other times, we are like the Grand Old Duke of York in the children's nursery rhyme, neither up nor down!

We can face the future with a high level of confidence because our long-term destiny is not focused exclusively on who we are, but on who God is, as revealed in the cross of the Lord Jesus Christ. That really takes the pressure off us, and by the same token, it ensures all the glory goes to him.

When God spills out his wrath like a dam bursting its banks on the day of the Lord, it will not be coming in our direction; we are safe and secure in Christ. And when he empties out his final wrath in eternal hell, it will not have our name written on it either. It is not our portion. It is not what we have been chosen to receive. It is not our divine allocation. Christ has already taken all of this for us! We shall miss it because we are gospel people, God's people.

Our salvation is wonderfully assured, it is a gilt-edged guarantee and nothing and no one can stop it coming to us (Romans 8:31-39). We are as sure of heaven today as if we were already there! We were once the children of wrath, but no more, now we are the sons of God! The full-blown fury of the anger of God will never land in our lap! We may have an appointment with death as intimated in Hebrews 9:27, but we do not have a date with the wrath of God. That is one divine attribute that we shall never have to face or contemplate since we are destined for the throne, born and bound for glory!

Life and death

It is thrilling to realise that our future prospects are all dependent on what Christ accomplished at Calvary. He died for us. It is personal, for he died with my best interests at heart. Similarly, he died on your behalf. To quote the hymn writer, Phillip P Bliss (1838-76), 'In my place condemned he stood, [he] sealed my pardon with his blood.' He gave his life as our substitute when he went to the cross as our representative. He did for us what we could never in a month of Sundays possibly do for ourselves. He died that we might live.

As John Stott says, 'Thus his death and our life are deliberately contrasted and inseparably connected.' Our life is due entirely to his death, and the kind of life he has won for us is a life lived 'together with him'. It can be explained like this, he died our death so that we might live his life! This is tremendous, for through his death we have not only been reprieved, but reconciled! He not only let us off the hook, he let us in to his family!

And all the manifold blessings of this life with him will be ours whether, at his advent, we are awake or asleep. Christ wants us, dead or alive, we do not miss out either way! That is Paul's inimitable way of getting back to the nitty-gritty of what was really bothering the believers in first-century Thessalonica. In life and in death we participate fully in the abundant life we have in Jesus Christ. In a word, Paul says, be alive, because Jesus died for us at Calvary. Whether we live or die, we enjoy the presence of the Lord. Life with a capital L. Paul encourages us to live with eternity in view. This is what living expectantly is all about, it is living in the future tense. When we live this way, we will be mentally active, spiritually alert, and prophetically aware.

5:11

Getting alongside people

In a final attempt to rally the troops, Paul says, *encourage one another and build one another up.* It is so easy to lose sight of God's perspective. Not unlike Winnie-the-Pooh whose favourite pastime is to put his head in the honey jar. A beautiful analogy. Most of us enjoy deliciously sweet things. I do! Solomon writes that 'gracious words are like a honeycomb, sweetness to the soul and health to the body'

(Proverbs 16:24). To what extent are we using words to build one another up? Keep your head, including your mouth, in a honey jar!

Think about it, try to visualise someone in your mind's eye who is discouraged or anxious, someone who is physically ill at home or in hospital, someone who is always giving out, someone who is lonely or spiritually drifting. What can we say to encourage such a person? And how will we say it to them when God gives us that golden opportunity?

Most of us realise that this world is no friend to the people of God. It can be a tough, unforgiving place, as many of us know to our cost. It is so easy to get hurt and chivvied by it. That is where the local gospel church is different: it should be a lush oasis in the middle of a sandy desert, a rest stop in the marathon of life, a honey jar in the dark forest, a community of mutual support. We are in it together and we owe it to each other to share one another's burdens and joys.

Paul's careful use of the word *another* is designed to emphasise the reciprocal nature of Christian care. It is a two-way thing! We are not to leave it to an elite of professional counsellors. Sure, they have an important job to do and sometimes they are essential, but caring and encouraging one another are ministries that belong to all members of the body of Christ. The ministry of encouragement is like oxygen to the followers of Jesus.

In one *Peanuts* storyline, Linus has just written a comic strip of his own and he craves Lucy's opinion:

Frame 1: Linus tentatively hands Lucy his comic strip and says, 'Lucy, would you read this and tell me if you think it's funny?'

Frame 2: Lucy pats her foot, and a bit of a grin comes across her face. She looks at Linus and says, 'Well, Linus, who wrote this?' Linus with his chest heaved out and a great big smile says, 'Lucy, I wrote that.'

Frame 3: Lucy crumples it up, throws it to the side, and says, 'Well, then, I don't think it's very funny.'

Frame 4: Linus picks up his comic strip, throws his blanket over his shoulder, looks at Lucy and says, 'Big sisters are the crab grass in the lawn of life.'

Such is life sometimes, even in a local congregation. We can easily be the crab grass in the manicured lawn of somebody else's life. No wonder Paul encourages us to be positive in our relationships.

5:12

Leadership in the local church

It was the leadership guru John Maxwell who said that 'coming together is a beginning. Keeping together is progress. Working together is success.' This theme is immensely important to the Thessalonian believers. In fact, it is not only apposite to them, it is right up-to-date for your church and mine, two thousand years down the road. It is just so practical and down-to-earth that it takes the wind out of our sails. Paul gives us a set of crisp, clear guidelines to follow which will enable us to maintain purity in our gospel fellowship. It is not just a matter of believing sound doctrine, or crossing our theological Ts, or preaching the whole counsel of God. It is more! Much more!

Our lives should be a reflection of the beauty and loveliness of Jesus. God could have used mirrors to reflect his person, but he did not. He could have sent angels to reveal his character, but he did not. He gave that indescribable privilege to his children, to us. Therefore, says Paul, we should be examples of godliness to those all around us.

Paul indicates to us how fellowship can be deepened, and at times, damaged. He shows us that we have a solemn responsibility to each other in the Lord because we are members of the same family. So when we opt out of our responsibilities to each other, and neglect to care for each other with a heartfelt compassion, and ignore the principles God has set down, how terribly sad it all is! Each of us is like a wheelbarrow full of loose bricks, we are dependent on the skilful hands of others to build us up and help us see the mortar of the clear-cut truth of God's love.

We are meant to be brothers and sisters, bonded together in Christ. Paul has said it before, and he says it again, we are family! A gospel family. We need to face up to the fact that no earthly family is perfect. And, dare I say it, no church family is perfect either. There are problems in every company of the Lord's people. It is just that some are much more serious than others. Some appear to be trivial and insignificant. Others look as though they are insurmountable and Everest-like. However, at the end of every day, whatever the nettlesome issue at stake, we are still part of a family.

Happy families

A happy family is a priceless blessing. Not just a card game! With that in mind, what are the essentials for a happy church family? What are the ingredients for a warm, vibrant, gospel church? It seems to me that where there is love and care and understanding, where there is a sense of mutual help and healthy respect, where there is a tough but tender form of discipline, all these combine to bring immense joy and stability to the family of God.

How will this be seen? It will be evident in our attitude to one another in private and public. It will be seen in the various activities, inside and outside church, in which we are involved. It will be highlighted in our affinity with the Lord Jesus. That explains why Paul moves slowly but surely in this minisection, dealing tactfully with two main areas of truth which are both hypersensitive matters. When he feels the need to give them a piece of his mind, he does so; when he reckons they need a chunk of his heart, he does that as well. Either way, he handles the obvious difficulties and potential fallout with an extremely delicate touch, not like a bull in a china shop!

The preacher is talking about our conduct and composure in the local church. We have no idea what prompted Paul to write in the manner in which he did. We do know that the Thessalonian church had responsible leaders, since Luke singles out Aristarchus and Secundus for special mention in

Acts 20:4. The likelihood is that some church members were feeling a bit peeved and had been disrespectful towards their leaders; the chances are they had directed towards them some stinging criticism. On the other hand, some of the leadership team may have provoked this reaction by their heavy-handed or autocratic behaviour.

Quite frankly, we are whistling in the wind for we do not know the prime reason for the backlash. I can only imagine that a lot of it can be attributed to sore feelings of hurt pride because someone tramped on someone else's toes. And they picked the ones with big juicy corns! The common denominator is that Paul rejected both attitudes as totally unacceptable behaviour.

Leaders lead

Paul makes it very clear that churches should enjoy the rich benefit of pastoral oversight but, as John Stott suggests, 'they are not meant to monopolise ministries, but rather to multiply them!' We must never forget that God has ordained leadership for every local assembly of his people. That is why we have elders and deacons, Spirit-filled individuals who lead the flock of God in a way that is God-glorifying.

Those involved in such leadership roles should be men of vision as well as being those who can sell that vision to others. They need to be flexible and able to adapt to the changing needs of a given situation. They are not those who dig their heels in, nor do they drag their heels either. Spiritual discernment is an absolute must, as is the ability to make and take decisions. We are talking here about people who will act, not always react. It is all about leaders who lead from the front, and at the same time, still retain the spirit of a servant. Servant leadership. The Jesus model.

They should be men of prayer whose life is in touch and in tune with the Lord: men who have a heart for God and a big heart for his people; men who can see the big picture in relation to the purpose of God for the world and for his people in the world. In the final analysis, we are looking for men of God, men of the word of God. When we have good, godly, gifted, gospel people in positions of leadership we should respond to them in a threefold manner.

Leaders ... where the action is

We should *respect* them! Two vitally important phrases provide the basis for such a healthy respect, *among you* and *over you*. The underlying concept is this:

- As a leader, they are *over* us.
- As a brother, they are *among* us.

Our respect for them should be based on the fact that even though they are our leaders, they are still our brothers. It is apparent that there is a minimum of three areas in which they are deserving of our loyal support. The first is in relation to their activity. All those in positions of leadership are meant to be workers not passengers, team players not spectators. They are supposed to be down on the field of play, not standing on the terraces cheering or complaining.

According to Paul, they should be those who *work hard*. I can tell you from years of experience, this is not a Sunday-only, one-day-a-week job! I love what C H Spurgeon once said about his own ministry. He said, 'I work myself to death and pray myself alive again!' This is a service that at times can be so wearisome, tiring, and demanding that we fall into bed at night exhausted. The word that Paul used conjures up a picture of rippling muscles and pouring sweat. Paul applied it to farm labourers and to the physical exertions of his own tent making (2 Timothy 2:6). He also used it in relation to his apostolic labours as in 1 Timothy 4:10, and to the sheer hard work of his dedicated colleagues as in Romans 16:12. He linked it in with those who labour in preaching and teaching as in 1 Timothy 5:17.

Shepherding is no easy task, it is an arduous role. There are buckets of tears to shed, as well as sackfuls of joys to share. There are many ups and downs. There is that which is conducted upfront, but often there is so much more carried out behind the scenes. The average person in the pew has little or no idea of what goes on beyond the glare of the public eye, which is probably a good thing.

Leaders ... carry the can

We respect them because of their authority, it is President Harry Truman's 'the buck stops here' syndrome. A similar argument is advanced by the anonymous writer when he says, 'Remember your leaders, those who spoke to you the word of God. Consider the outcome of their way of life and imitate their faith … Obey your leaders and submit to them, for they are keeping watch over your souls, as those who will have to give an account. Let them do this with joy and not with groaning, for that would be of no advantage to you' (Hebrews 13:7, 17).

Those men privileged to exercise leadership of a pastoral nature have a solemn responsibility as they invest their lives in caring for others. They have the superintending role of an overseer in that they watch over people. Among other duties, they are to:

- Feed the flock with the truth of God's word.
- Lead the flock by example and testimony.
- Plead for the flock before the throne of grace.

Such an anointed individual is in touch with the living God, in touch with reality, and in touch with the people to whom the Lord has called him to minister. He will have both eyes wide open as he constantly scans the congregation to see how folk in the pew are getting along in their relationship with the Lord. Inevitably, as an undershepherd, it means going after those sheep that have strayed because the grass looked greener on the wrong side of the fence, and picking up those that have been wounded along the journey.

Why bother? Because one day, at the judgment seat of Christ, leaders will give a full, factual account of their time spent in that congregation. And when they do, they want to be able to do it with a big smile rather than a doleful grunt.

The verdict of the Lord Jesus on this God-driven style of ministry is best summed up in the one liner, 'I am among you as the one who serves' (Luke 22:27).

The elders who oversee gospel congregations have no justification for behaving like Protestant mini-popes, or adopting the Rambo style of much secular management that insists on the right to manage, often to the detriment of its workforce – 'Do as I say, not as I do!' What Jesus advocates, and Paul stands shoulder-to-shoulder with him, is a servant leadership where humility and gentleness are the dominant features. Jesus-style leadership is best seen when we take a basin of water and a towel and wash other people's smelly feet (John 13:1-17).

Leaders ... talk the talk

An elder or a leader will always be able and willing to sit down with the people of God and open up the word of God to them (1 Timothy 3:2). Paul speaks at the end of verse 12 of those who *admonish you*. It portrays an ongoing ministry where a motley group of believers are consistently reminded, personally and corporately, of biblical truth. It is all about teaching and applying Scripture in a collective sense and that is supremely important, but it should also incorporate those times when individuals are discipled on a one-to-one basis.

The Greek word for *admonish* is more often than not used in an ethical context, and it generally means to warn against bad behaviour and its tragic consequences. Yes, there are times when leaders need to crack the whip. It is the kind of necessary instruction that might be given to someone who is in serious danger of going off the rails. Being a negative word, it is often coupled with teaching as in Colossians 1:28 and 3:16.

Both these vital roles belong to the brief of those in pastoral leadership, implying that good elders are not spineless or toothless individuals. I hasten to add that such a word does not denote a harsh Draconian-type ministry. Leon Morris makes that point, 'While its tone is brotherly, it is big-brotherly.' This is not big-brotherly in the Orwellian sense of the phrase, but in the sense of having someone in the church leadership who is genuinely looking after our spiritual interests. There is no need for us to smell a rat, for this is not an old style, red flag, totalitarian regime; rather, it is total care within the family of believers.

What attitude should the members of a gospel church adopt towards those in leadership? 'They are neither to despise them, as if they were dispensable, nor to flatter or fawn on them as if they were popes or princes, but rather to respect them, and to hold them in the highest regard in love because of their work,' notes John Stott. This combination of appreciation and affection will enable pastors and the people they lead to serve and live in peace with each other.

5:13

Roast pastor for Sunday lunch

In saying what he does, Paul takes the whole matter a logical step forward. We should appreciate these people for what they do for us, and at the same time, we should also show our affection for them in the Lord when we *esteem them very highly in love because of their work.*

Ever wondered why there should be such a refreshingly positive response to them? Why should we back them and bless them? The answer is found in Paul's teaching in Ephesians 4:11-13. There we are reminded that their gift of leadership is from the Lord, and from God's perspective, a pastor is also his gift to his church. Therefore, all those in Christian leadership should never be taken for granted.

Sadly, it does not always happen that way. I certainly know, and you probably know as well, of situations where pastor and people are constantly on a war footing. To put it simply, they are at loggerheads with one another. An unhappy experience like that does little or nothing for the glory of God. It is incredibly painful for all those unfortunate enough to be caught in the crossfire between the rival factions. It massively inhibits the church's life and growth, as well as seriously damaging the church's public image. When churches pass through traumatic times of upheaval and disunity it often has long-term repercussions that we fail to realise. You see, bipolar unity is not unity at all. That reiterates what Paul is saying, we should always endeavour to see the goodness and grace of God in the lives of those holding down leadership positions. By the same token, we should do all in our power to stand by them and encourage them in the work they are doing.

John Stott sums it up so well when he acknowledges, 'Happy is the local church family in which pastors and people recognise that God calls different believers to different ministries, exercise their own ministries with diligence and humility, and give to others the respect and love which their God-appointed labour demands!'

LIP ... Live In Peace

The third facet of Paul's thinking in relation to our attitude to leaders is that we should genuinely thank God for them. This is the fundamental thought behind Paul's comment, *be at peace among yourselves*. A most unusual kind of phrase to use in this context! It appears strangely out of place. Well, nothing could be further from the truth. Paul has been around long enough to know what goes on in churches, he knows what happens behind closed doors, he knows what takes place in the rough and tumble of everyday life in the average congregation. Someone has said that 'church would be easy if it weren't for people!' Paul knows that the church 'is a melting pot of ethnic diversity, various socio-economic statuses, and very opinionated people,' suggests Mark Howell.

Sure, it is a fact of life that we do not always agree with those in leadership roles; we do not always see eye to eye with them. There will be things they do and things they do not do, that to be honest, we just do not like. But, says Paul, in light of eternity, those differences do not matter. In spite of how we feel at a given point in time, we still owe it to them, to the wider inclusive church family, and to the Lord, to sincerely thank God for them. Why? Because of what they are and who they are. We have gone full circle!

5:14

Dealing with problem children

It is a fair comment to make that we get all sorts of sheep in a flock. Sheep are oftentimes noisy, dirty, stupid animals who follow each other's lead and react to danger with confusion. Without pushing the comparison too far, we get all kinds of people in a church fellowship. There is the infamous trio of yelpers, helpers, and skelpers! They have often been described as the so-wise, the unwise, and the otherwise! It was Adoniram Judson Gordon (1836-95), founder of Gordon-Conwell Theological Seminary, who classified church members as figureheads, soreheads, and deadheads. I would be inclined to add another to his list: hotheads!

In the previous section, the focus was on the leaders, and that is hugely important because things have to be right, at the top. Now, in these verses, Paul widens the net and talks about the rest of us lesser mortals as he reminds us that we all have a distinctive ministry to one another. This is how the body of Christ is really meant to function. As Philip Arthur says, with keen insight into the problem, 'As far as Paul is concerned, these vital pastoral tasks were not the sole province of the top tier of church leadership. One certain way of ensuring that the job is done badly is to leave it to those in oversight positions. There is simply too much to be done!'

Without doubt, such a key ministry is the responsibility of the church membership at large, and consists of the members of the body of Christ having a mutual care and concern for each other. In this instance, there is much more needed than nice thoughts, pious platitudes, and weasel words. Care and concern require robust action. Paul does not mince his words when he lays down the law with four commands to take on board.

- *Admonish the idle* ... the 'won't dos' whatever!

This refers to those pew-warming believers who are blithe when it comes to fulfilling their church responsibilities. They are careless. Stubborn. Out of step with the leadership. Out of line with the word of God. It is not unreasonable to assume that they are the same lackadaisical, what-right-have-you-got-to-tell-me-what-to-do people breaking rank with the rest of the church fellowship, as well as the leadership.

Our initial response is relatively straightforward, for they are to be reprimanded in love. It is hard to say it, and even more difficult to do it; but there are times when it is necessary to confront others with the truth so that their rebellious behaviour might be corrected. Bearing in mind Galatians 6:1, there is a place to do it, a time to do it, and a proper way to do it. These are the hard-hearted people in the congregation.

- *Encourage the faint-hearted* ... the 'want tos' however!

We are to come alongside and draw near to those saints who get down in the dumps rather easily. There is a time for getting close to people. We are to encourage those who are prone to give up and those who are tempted to give in;

we are to try and lift them up. This may involve us giving them a few words of comfort, or offering to them a pair of listening ears. It may even mean that we just show them in some other concrete way that someone genuinely cares for them and about them. By its very nature, this is a hands-on approach that Paul is advocating.

There are always quitters in every church family; a sad fact of life, but unfortunately, all too true to life. The baseline is that it is always too soon to quit. For whatever reason, there are those who perpetually look on the dark side, Paul wants us to show them the sunny side up. These are the faint-hearted people in the church.

- *Help the weak* ... the 'can't dos' whenever!

The verb for *help* presents a graphic picture of the undergirding that those who are weak need. It is as if Paul wrote to the stronger Christians and said to them, 'Hold on to them, cling to them, even put your arm around them!' Ours is a support ministry, in the best sense of that word, as the reference here is to those who are weak in the faith. They have not grown up in their relationship with the Lord. They are still on the milk when they should really be eating and enjoying the meat of the word of God. To all such, Paul says, we should hold on to them, bear them up, care for them, stand by them, and stand with them for as long as it takes to see them through. I suppose we could say that these dear friends are numbered among the broken-hearted. As Michael Martin so aptly puts it, 'The church should support these weak brothers as beloved fellow strugglers, not desert them as ignorant or unimportant stragglers.'

Charles Dickens (1812-70) was right when he said that 'no one is useless in this world who lightens the burden of it to anyone else.' These three categories of people could be easily described as the problem children of the church family, and take it from me, every gospel church has them. Some more than others! Part of the problem is their spiritual diet, for they are feeding their soul on trivialities, titbits, and takeaways. Nothing substantial. Plenty to lick their lips about, but nothing to sink their teeth into. None of us will grow big in God if we seek to exist on spiritual junk food; what I call the McDonaldisation of the church.

Patience is a virtue

That is why the final arrow in Paul's quiver is mega important when he challenges us to *be patient with them all*. We have seen it so often before, and here we see it again, Paul is a realist.

- An optimist sees only opportunities.
- A pessimist sees only problems.
- A realist sees the opportunities presented by problems!

The travelling preacher does not run around with his head in the clouds; he is a down-to-earth bloke. He knows this will not be easy, for there will be many times when we are pushed beyond our limit, when we have just about had enough and feel as though we can take no more, when we have that sinking sensation in the pit of our stomach. In such moments when we are pulling out our hair, Paul suggests that we need to think outside the box and be patient and give these folk who are driving us round the bend some quality time and show them Jesus.

It appears that the apostle is exhorting us to be long-tempered (as opposed to short-tempered) for that is the accepted meaning of the Greek term for 'patience'. This wonderful virtue is an attribute of God, as we see in Exodus 34:6, Psalm 103:8, and Joel 2:13. It is also a fruit of the Spirit and a top characteristic of love, as in Galatians 5:22 and 1 Corinthians 13:4. The bottom line is this: since God has been infinitely patient with us, we too must be patient with others.

It conveys the idea of being tough and durable in the face of stiff, unrelenting, intense pressure. It is manifesting a quiet, steady strength that can handle the stress and strain; it is being able to cope with very real feelings of disappointment, hardship, and pain. When push comes to shove, it is all about self-control, for God does not want us to operate with a short fuse. He does not expect us to sit on a time bomb! People can be so discouraging, for they promise so much, only to disappoint, and in situations like that, it would be so easy to throw in the towel. That is the last thing we want to do, for the church must never be the kind of army that shoots its wounded!

It is helpful to realise that woven into the fabric of this brief section is the thought that we should always watch our motives. Sure, this is what happens in a family and this is what happens in a local church. Human nature, we say. It may be human, but it is also sinful. And such behaviour can never be swept under the carpet!

5:15

Getting even

'I will never permit any man to narrow and degrade my soul by making me hate him,' writes Booker T Washington (1856-1915). That is why Paul says, *See that no one repays evil for evil, but always seek to do good to one another and to everyone.* Here is an allusion both to the teaching of Jesus in the Sermon on the Mount (Matthew 5:43-48) and to his own refusal to hit back which we read of in 1 Peter 2:20. Paul is simply saying that we should never retaliate and try to get even with a brother or sister. There is no loophole, no get-out clause, in the wording of Paul's injunction.

We should be careful what we return to them, no matter what missile they have fired our way. The temptation is for us to want to get our own back, we want to stand up for our own rights, we want to take everything into our own hands and settle old scores. A gospel church should be a place where kindness and generosity flourishes, not a battleground for getting even! In divine maths, two wrongs never make one right!

A mother ran into the bedroom when she heard her seven-year-old son scream. She found his two-year-old sister pulling his hair. She gently released the girl's grip and said comfortingly to the boy, 'There, there. She didn't mean it. She doesn't know that hurts.' He nodded his acknowledgement, and she left the room. As she started down the hall the girl yelled at the top of her voice. Rushing back in, she asked, 'What happened?' The boy replied, 'She knows now!'

We should endeavour to be genial and considerate and only do what is good, as ultimately, this is the only way to overcome evil. So I am suggesting we adopt a radical approach that is not out of this world, but it is straight out of the word of God! Maybe we need to ask ourselves the question: WWJD? What would Jesus do? His way may not be the easy way, but it is always the best way.

We should be an integral part of the solution, rather than exacerbating the problem. Better to be effective extinguishers, rather than putting more fuel on the fire. In today's litigious society, we in the church are here to build bridges, not set up barricades. It is the mindset that turns the other cheek and says, I want to help you, not one that reacts with hostility and declares, I am going to sue you!

When we find ourselves in explosive situations like those mentioned above, we should show the love of Jesus to those people who get under our skin and cause us enormous frustration. It is good to remember that God always has the last word. In the book of our lives, he alone writes the last chapter. We should be happy and content, therefore, to leave it all with him.

'Good for good, evil for evil: that is natural.
Evil for good: that is devilish.
Good for evil: that is divine.' (Saint Augustine, 354-430)

Smoothing the ragged edge

All that Paul has been saying in this section is appropriate for every gospel church, and in many ways, what we have here is a beautiful vision of the local church as a community, not only of mutual comfort and encouragement, but of mutual forbearance and service as well.

> 'Lord, you have searched me, you know me; Lord, help me be the kind of person you want me to be! Lord, let the beauty of Jesus be seen in me ... Lord, let there be love shared among us ... Lord, bind us together with cords that cannot be broken.'

We know what happens when God answers that prayer in our lives, there is a minimum of two results: we respect our rulers; and our behaviour among the brethren will bring glory and praise to the peerless name of Jesus.

5:16

Staccato sayings

No matter what angle we view it from, the emphasis from here on in is on practical Christianity that is geared to living for God in the here and now. Candid comments. Paul is not sitting like some bespectacled professor in an ivory tower, he is on the level. Here is distilled wisdom at its finest and best. We are meant to enjoy life, not endure it!

In this paragraph there are seven sayings that give us a life permeated with rapturous joy and zest. The most magnetic people on earth should be those in the family of

God, for their experience of the grace of God is invigorating, astounding, and contagious. It knocks us sideways, such is its amazing power. It sweeps us along on a tidal wave of blessing. In Christ alone, we have something to sing and shout about. We have every reason to be infectious in our unbridled enthusiasm for the Lord.

This closing section reminds us that we can experience life to the full if we embrace and personalise these seven pertinent, pithy sayings. Richard Mayhue writes, 'These short statements strike at the very heart of the Christian life; each is a command that expects obedience; these imperatives could be viewed as the ABCs of Christian living.'

Joy 24/7

The first, *rejoice always*, extols the delights of a life in tune with the Lord. This is the shortest verse in the Greek New Testament. It means we have something in our spirit that the world does not have. We have a joy, deep down in our heart. In the first half of the twentieth century, Billy Sunday (1862-1935) was America's best-known evangelist and revivalist. A firebrand preacher, he quipped in one sermon, 'If you have no joy, there's a leak in your Christianity somewhere!'

I heard a brother make a shrewd, tongue-in-cheek observation on one occasion, that some of God's people have a joy that is so deep it never rises to the surface! Happiness depends on what happens to us and what is taking place around us, but this joy is centred in Christ. Our circumstances change, the tide of events ebbs and flows, our fortunes fluctuate as they rise and fall, our emotions can be like the proverbial yo-yo; yet, even when life goes flip-flop, we still have a joy in our hearts: 24 hours a day, 7 days a week. Not just some of the time, or most of the time, but all of the time. It was Sebastien Chamfort (1741-94) who said, 'The most wasted of all our days are those in which we have not laughed.'

We noted in Paul's greeting to the church that Christ gives us his peace and his grace; here it is his joy that is imparted to us. This exquisite blessing is ours when we abide in him (John 15:1-11). When our lives are lived in the fulness of the Holy Spirit, then joy is a fruit much in evidence (Galatians 5:22). Paul taps in to what the psalmist invited God's people to do years earlier, for we read, 'Come, let us sing for joy to the Lord; let us shout aloud to the Rock of our salvation' (Psalm 95:1, NIV). In another Psalm, the Old Hundredth, he says, 'Shout for joy to the Lord, all the earth.' We shout for joy for there is exuberance in knowing and worshipping the risen Lord Jesus!

In the context of the local church meeting, Paul is issuing not an order to be happy, but an invitation to joyful, vibrant, lively worship. So many of our church services tend to be unforgivably gloomy and boring; when we walk through the glass doors, it seems as though we are walking into a morgue, for people are so doleful and apathetic. We start at 11.00 sharp and end at 12.15 dull! Our penance is over! There is no need to be like that! Our times of worship should be a celebration of felicity and faith, a joyful rehearsal of what God has done and given us through the Lord Jesus Christ. At the same time, there is no need to go over the top and swing from the crystal chandeliers in the sanctuary or dance up and down the plush carpeted aisles, for we need to recognise that, as we engage our hearts and voices in worship, we do so with a sense of reverence, awe, and humility.

5:17

Staying in touch

The apostle highlights the desirability of a life lived in touch with the Lord, and the futility of leaving God out. *Pray without ceasing* underlines the necessity of keeping short accounts with the Lord. If there is one thing we all agree on, it is that God wants us to pray. The idea is not round-the-clock praying where we are never off our knees, for that is impossible, unrealistic, and unworkable. The idea includes praying in the shower, at mealtimes, while working, in the car … . Heaven knows we need it in the car sometimes!

Staying in close touch with God is what Paul has in mind. It is an experience where we are never offline. We have always-on messaging, to use today's communication parlance. It is essential that we keep the lines open and ensure the proper channels are always clear; it does not work if there is a blockage between our hearts and heaven. It is being able to converse and chat with the Lord at any time of day or night. To all intents and purposes, we have a hotline to heaven. 'Prayer is a shield to the soul, a sacrifice to God, and a scourge to Satan,' is the observation of John Bunyan.

A prayerful attitude like this means we consciously live in the atmosphere of Christ and breathe in the rarefied air of heaven. It is experiencing the reality of Psalm 91:1, for we 'abide in the shadow of the Almighty'. Nehemiah knew all about it; at the same time as he was thinking on his feet, he was sending a quick prayer up to heaven (2:4). Before King Artaxerxes, he could identify with George Failing when he said, 'He who does not pray when the sun shines will not know how to pray when the clouds roll in.'

Such moments are times when we sense his nearness, and live in the place where God answers prayer. The Lord is only a prayer away, he sees our every sigh, he hears our every sob, he is familiar with every sentence we utter. That is what fellowship with the Father is all about. We get rid of the burdens as we hand them over to him. And when we do that, we find release in our heart, and as a consequence, joy abounds. Because prayer frees us from the anchors of life that drag us down and drain our joy. He is El Shaddai, the God who is just what we need, the God who is enough. Exciting! And humbling. Corrie ten Boom posed the question: 'Is prayer your steering wheel or spare tyre?'

Can't pray, won't pray

It needs to be emphasised that Paul is not only speaking about our personal prayer life, the general context would lend a fair amount of weight to it being corporate prayer. The depressing experience of many gospel churches is that the prayer meeting is either a relic of the distant past, or else it is the worst attended meeting in the course of an average week. For reasons best known to themselves, people refuse to turn up for a Wednesday night prayer meeting!

If praise and worship is so important that we push it to the top of our agenda, surely prayer is compellingly indispensable! It is crucial to the church's ongoing impact in the community that we make time to pray with one another. Serious intercession should be the hallmark of a gospel ministry, the life and soul of a spiritually healthy congregation. A biblical ministry that is signally blessed is usually one underpinned with prayer.

John Stott reminds us that 'we should be praying for our own church members, far and near; we should be praying for the church throughout the world, its leaders, its adherence to the truth of God's revelation, its holiness, its unity, and its mission; we should be praying for our nation, our parliament, and our government, and for a just, free, compassionate, and participatory society; we should be praying for world mission, especially for places and peoples resistant to the gospel; we should be praying for peace, justice, and environmental stewardship; and we should be praying for the poor, the oppressed, the hungry, the homeless, and the sick.'

Stott offers this challenging comment by way of conclusion when he genuinely wonders 'if the comparatively slow progress towards world peace, world equity, and world evangelisation is not due, more than anything else, to the prayerlessness of the people of God.' I imagine, in fact I know, that there is more than a grain of truth in his analysis of the situation as it stands at present.

5:18

An attitude of gratitude

'Some people are always grumbling because roses have thorns,' noted Jean-Baptiste Alphonse Karr, 'I am thankful that thorns have roses.' The third of Paul's sayings is where he proposes that we express our bowled-over sense of gratitude to the Lord, when he writes, *give thanks in all circumstances; for this is the will of God in Christ Jesus for you.*

Thankfulness should always characterise the Christian as he says to himself, 'Bless the Lord, O my soul, and forget not all his benefits' (Psalm 103:2). Even a grumpy old man like Jeremiah recognised the truth that 'the steadfast love of the Lord never ceases; his mercies never come to an end; they are new every morning' (Lamentations 3:22-23). When we give thanks in all circumstances – the good, the very good, and the not so good – we are manifesting the gift and grace of contentment. In other words, we are happy with our portion in life. OK, maybe it could be better, but it could also be an awful lot worse!

I read of an interview with a balloonist who was grounded by appalling weather at an international ballooning festival. When asked if he was disappointed, he said, 'I would rather be on the ground wishing I was in the air than be in the air wishing I was on the ground.'

- Thanks *for* everything. No!
- Thanks *in* everything. Yes!

A superb example that springs to mind is the story of Paul when he found himself in a rat-infested Philippian prison. He did not sit around bemoaning his lot; he was not complaining about all that happened to him; he did not whinge about human rights or carp on because he was denied access to his attorney; he did not get all worked up into a feeling sorry for himself kind of frenzy. Instead, he praised the Lord in his dank, underground cell, an eloquent tribute to the grace and faithfulness of God.

You see, whether we find ourselves in the storm or in the calm, in deep waters or on dry land, it matters not, for his sovereign plan is designed for our good. This is what living in the reality of Romans 8:28 and Ecclesiastes 7:14 is all about; this is what enables us to say a sincere 'thank you' for every experience he brings into our lives. In the best of times and worst of times, we say 'thank you' to a loving heavenly Father, for he knows best! As John Stott remarks, 'It is not by accident that in Greek one and the same noun – *charis* – does duty for both "grace" and "gratitude".'

The least we can do is submit willingly to his gracious providence with an overwhelming sense of gratefulness. That is the grace of gratitude – the Habakkuk principle (Habakkuk 3:17-19). The Christian's life is to be an unceasing eucharist. That helps crystallise what our response ought to be to all that life throws at us. The Lord appreciates and values people with thankful hearts! When all is said and done, such a mindset blends in beautifully with his perfect will for our lives. Again, Horatius Bonar comes to our aid:

Fill thou my life, O Lord my God,
In every part with praise,
That my whole being may proclaim
Thy being and thy ways.

Praise in the common things of life,
Its goings out and in;
Praise in each duty and each deed,
However small and mean.

Ellen Decker tells the story of her son Ryan who, when he was a five-year-old, offered the following prayer during family devotions: 'Dear Jesus, sorry for the mess we made in the yard today.' After a slight pause, he concluded, 'Thank you for the fun we had doing it!'

5:19

On fire for God

Number four of seven is a life on top for the Lord. That may seem an unusual phrase but when we see what Paul says, it all fits together neatly, *Do not quench the Spirit.* We know from Ephesians 4:30 that the Holy Spirit is a friend: we grieve him when we hurt him. In this instance, he is likened to a fire: we quench him when we suppress him and stifle his influence in our lives. Here is an impassioned plea for us to acknowledge the sovereignty and freedom of the Holy Spirit.

The danger is that we may try to extinguish him in our lives and ministry. It is foolish to pour cold water on the fire of his plan for our lives, or even to dampen the effect of his word upon our hearts. The fire burns up the dross in that it purifies us. It has incredible power so that it brings light and gives warmth. Perhaps more than ever, we need the Isaiah experience, to be touched with a live coal from the altar and be a people ignited for the Lord (Isaiah 6:6-7). It cleansed Isaiah's mouth! We need to burn for the Lord in such a manner that men and women will be aware that we are ablaze for him. On fire for God. Irish missionary to India, Amy Carmichael (1867-1951), prayed, 'Make me thy fuel, O flame of God.'

5:20

When familiarity breeds contempt

Item number five on Paul's agenda is a life being taught by the Lord, *do not despise prophecies*. When the Lord is speaking to his people through his word, we should be extra cautious about our response. We must never downgrade it; we must never devalue the word from the Lord by displaying an apparent lack of interest in it or by giving it a cool, frosty reception. When biblical truth is proclaimed, whatever the channel, we should treat it as the word of God: it is not the voice of man; it is the living God who is speaking to us. Let us not get overly familiar with him and his word for when we do we risk bringing contempt to our souls.

This injunction was especially relevant in the early church when they did not have the complete canon of Scripture as we have today. That meant there were those in the congregation whom the Lord raised up with a gift of prophecy, men and women who knew and spoke God's mind and will. In our day, we have no need for this role, for we have the mind and heart of God revealed in the word of God; in the sixty-six books which make up the Bible, we have a full and final revelation of God to his people.

To add to it or take from it is just not permissible and there are many serious warnings sprinkled throughout the Bible with regard to such an arrogant attitude (Revelation 22:18-19). It is a total non-starter, for no one has the right or authority to tamper with the truth of Scripture. So, says Paul, when God is speaking into our situation and when the Lord is addressing our hearts through his word, be more than just a good listener, be a good hearer!

5:21

Litmus test

A radical call for spiritual discernment is Paul's sixth saying, when he urges us to engage our mind in a life of testing for the Lord, hence the statement, *test everything; hold fast what is good*. There is, especially in these critical days, a need for us to examine what is before us, by asking the searching question: Is this in harmony with the teaching of Scripture?

We need a mix of spiritual perception and biblical insight so that we may be able to distinguish the difference between what is right and wrong. Be discriminating, for all that glitters is not gold. We need to sift, evaluate, and weigh up carefully all that is said. The preacher man warmly recommends intelligent scrutiny.

The tendency in some circles is to write everything off that is branded 'new', and not content with that, to go on and throw the baby out with the bath water. We often say, 'that is not the way my father did it', meaning our earthly fathers. We need to be open-minded to new thoughts if they are scripturally sound. We must be prayerful in our approach and balanced in our critique of what is presented to us. Yes, we test it for the Lord, and we hold on to what is good. That means we take on board all that is authentic. We do not fall for the counterfeit, we see through that and go for the genuine article! It is the Berean syndrome (Acts 17:11).

There are many ways we can test what is being said; the most obvious is the test of Scripture. Does what is being said tally with the rest of Scripture? Another way concerns the person of our Lord Jesus Christ. Is this preaching an authentic Jesus? Is it the Christ of Scripture? The fact is, no one truly inspired by the Holy Spirit would deny that Jesus Christ is the Son of God. After all, the supreme ministry of the Holy Spirit is to glorify Jesus, not to undermine him. Another test is the gospel test. We should ask, what does the preacher say about the way of salvation? Is it by faith alone, by grace alone, by Christ alone? If it is not, we close our ears to what is being said. The last big test is the test of integrity, for the lifestyle of the preacher should be in total sync with the message he is proclaiming. There should be no contradiction between what he is and what he says. He walks his talk.

5:22

Don't touch it with a barge pole

The last principle Paul talks about is a life of triumph in the Lord, when he exhorts us to *abstain from every form of evil*. The apostle is calling God's people to a life of total abstinence. That command does not only apply to the more obvious, well-publicised sins that hit the headlines in the tabloid press, but to every form of evil.

It is not just evil itself that we must avoid, but the very appearance of it. In other words, we should keep ourselves unspotted and untainted from that which is less than desirable. Do not get contaminated. Do not allow yourself to become polluted. As my mother used to say, 'If in doubt, don't do it; if there is any doubt, don't dabble in it.' If we question whether something is ethical, it almost certainly is not. Professor Verna Wright often said, 'Don't fasten your shoelaces in a strawberry field!' Why? Well, we would not want people to think we are stealing strawberries! We should not give Joe Public a chance to talk about us, nor should we give him an opportunity to point an accusing finger at us. It is sad, but many a good life has been wasted and many a testimony ruined because of a moment's indiscretion. Keep yourself from temptation. At the risk of sounding simplistic, if we cannot take Jesus with us, then we should not be there!

5:23

Paul's wish list

When we move into the final few verses in the chapter, Paul bids them a fond farewell. He just wants to say 'goodbye' but that has not been an easy thing for him to do. He found it enormously difficult. Actually, he took six verses to close his letter. Everything he said shows his deep affection for them. He talks about:

- a faithful God
- immensely loyal friends
- lasting grace, peace, and sanctification

Paul frames a double petition in his prayer when he highlights the standard that God expects of us, *Now may the God of peace himself sanctify you completely, and may your whole spirit and soul and body be kept blameless at the coming of our Lord Jesus Christ.* Paul reverts to a theme near and dear to his heart: holiness of life. He dealt with it in the preceding chapter by reminding them that this lifestyle was part and parcel of God's will for them, an integral component of God's overall purpose for them. Sanctification is becoming in practice what we already are in perfection.

Without doubt, standards are falling, the enemy has come in like a flood, and the banner of holiness to the Lord is rarely unfurled to the breeze. Yet God's word has not changed. Living as we do in a filthy, dirty world he expects each of us to live a holy life and display godly character.

Paul indicates that this deep and thorough work in the heart of the Christian is ascribed to God our Father. It is a divine work as he makes us more like Jesus. This is what being conformed to his image is all about (Romans 8:29). It is positional in that we have been once-and-for-all set apart for God (Hebrews 10:10). Then it is intensely practical as it is a daily dealing with our sin and a consequent growth in holiness (2 Corinthians 7:1). It is further described as that which is perfect, for in the bliss of eternity, we shall be forever like him (1 John 3:1-3). The expectation in our hearts that one day we shall see Jesus should be a spur to us to be the kind of people that God wants us to be. It should galvanise us and set our faith on fire.

Paul prays that he might sanctify us *completely*. The underlying thought is entire sanctification for it impacts our *spirit and soul and body*. It is when everything is under his influence and control, and our lives are totally yielded to him. Full surrender. It is, according to Robert Murray McCheyne, who died at the age of twenty-nine, 'God making us as holy as a saved sinner can be.' Charles Wesley's hymn surely finds an echo in each of our hearts:

Jesus, all-atoning Lamb,
Thine, and only thine, I am:
Take my body, spirit, soul;
Only thou possess the whole.

Shalom!

We are introduced to the living Lord as the *God of peace*.

This is one of the communicable attributes of God that Paul mentions, one of those qualities that he is happy to share with those of us who are numbered among his children. He is peace personified, and because he is who he is, we can know him personally, and when we do, we can also know his peace. You see, when he is not in control of our lives, we are restless, in turmoil, and tossed hither and thither in every direction. But when he is Lord and enthroned as King, there is an inner calm, a conscious resting in him, an inward quietness, and a real sense of tranquillity. There is nothing to disturb or distract us for we feel his peace and we know his peace.

When Paul expressed a desire for us to be blameless when we stand before the Lord Jesus Christ, it brings to mind some info I found online. Apparently, archaeologists have discovered tombstones from Thessalonica marked with the inscription 'blameless'. That is touching for it indicates the impact God's word had upon the early church in the first century. By the same token, I cannot think of a better way to live in the twenty-first century, nor can I think of a better way to die! We are blameless in God's eyes as soon as we accept Christ's salvation.

5:24

Faithful One

Paul exudes out-and-out confidence in the amazing ability of God when he writes, *He who calls you is faithful; he will surely do it*. Wow! If he said it, he will do it! What a staggering comment from Paul's pen! It is one of those 'precious and very great promises' that we read about in 2 Peter 1:4.

In essence, God upholds all those whom he calls, and he fulfils all that he has promised. When people are faced with this issue of holiness of life, they tend to say, 'Me, I can't live it. It's impossible for me to keep the standard he has set. It's too much, it's too high, it's way beyond me. I've tried and failed so many times.' Paul responds, 'All right, I hear what you're saying, but look to the Lord Jesus.'

Why should we turn our eyes toward him?

- He called us.

The general call in evangelism became personalised when we bowed the knee to Jesus. It became effectual when we said 'yes' to Jesus.

- He is faithful.

The faithfulness of God is such that the psalmist tells us it reaches even to the clouds (Psalm 36:5). Down through the generations, the Lord has remained loyal and true, and never once, not once, has he let his people down. Never has he gone back on his word. When we needed him most, was he conspicuous by his absence? No, he was always there. He has not failed us, he will not fail us, and he cannot fail us.

- He is infinitely powerful.

Paul says quite emphatically that *he will do it*. Think of all that he has done for us in the past and all that he is doing in us and through us in the present. If he has done it before, he can surely do it again. No problem to him! The unbelievably good news is that our ultimate security rests on the fact that God is reliable and keeps his promises. 'Having begun a good work in a person's life, there is no possibility that he will not honour his commitment and bring everything to a happy conclusion,' notes Philip Arthur.

Real worship

Why will he do it? Because he longs that we might be with him in his home forever. See the connection between this hugely positive affirmation of faith in a God who is able to do it and Paul's plea to them to be found blameless in the previous verse. Over there we shall worship him with clean hands and pure hearts, we shall see him in the beauty of his holiness and commune with him in spirit and in truth.

A former Archbishop of Canterbury, William Temple (1881-1944), said, 'Worship is to quicken the conscience by the holiness of God, it is to feed the mind with the truth of God, it is to purge the imagination by the beauty of God, it is to open up the heart to the love of God, and it is to devote the will to the purpose of God.'

Basically, that type of worship comes from the kind of person the Lord is looking for in today's world and today's church – an individual who knows, that when he gets home to glory, he will not be out of place worshipping in heaven!

5:25

Before the throne of God above

Paul opens his heart and with all the passion he can muster he makes a plea to the young church in Thessalonica, *Brothers, pray for us.* How unashamed the great man is of such a request, it flows naturally from his heart on to the papyrus. I wonder, how did people respond? What a direct challenge!

I imagine that many of the spiritual stalwarts would be thrilled to stand alongside him in prayer. Others were perhaps a bit more cynical and may even have questioned his motive: was he simply after the sympathy vote or trying to curry favour. And there were probably a few who did not take his request under their notice. At the end of the day it shows that we are all made of the same material and we cannot do without each other, especially when it comes to touching the throne. It is the power of effective kneeling.

Paul has assured them on numerous occasions of his many prayers for them down through the years, now he feels as though he needs them to intercede on his behalf. As John Stott says, 'This is a touching example of his personal humility and of the reciprocity of Christian fellowship.'

Prayer power

Think of his wonderful humility for he is a fully grown man. He is a seasoned campaigner when it comes to gospel ministry and 'he is standing in the need of prayer.' Paul is small enough to see his many shortcomings and big enough to beg for their prayerful buttress.

Think also of his open-book honesty for this is exactly the way that he feels. If he did not, he would not have asked them in the first place. It is genuine, real, and sincere. What a tremendous encouragement for them to feel that they had a vital part to play in Paul's ministry, and that his success or failure was dependent, at least in part, on their faithfulness in prayer.

I fear that all too often we are inclined to forget this! C H Spurgeon who preached to 6,000 souls each week during Queen Victoria's heyday was a man of remarkable gifts. He was also extremely careful to attribute the blessing that came upon his ministry to the fact that his church, the congregation that met in London's Metropolitan Tabernacle, gave itself to prayer. To Mr Spurgeon, that was the secret to his astronomic success; so far as he was concerned, the prayer meeting was the powerhouse!

5:26

Tactfully tactile

We are encouraged to *greet all the brothers with a holy kiss.* The customary greeting in the early church was for a man to greet another man with a kiss on the cheek or forehead. It was the same principle for the ladies in the congregation. It was culturally acceptable in his day, the proper thing to do. They were demonstrating their love for each other in the family of God (1 John 3:16-17). Sadly, some cults have used this verse as a justification to introduce lust into worship. In Paul's time, it was a genuine seal of their affection, and this gesture gave them an enhanced feeling of belonging to one another.

Today a big lot depends where we live, and to a greater or lesser degree, the kind of gospel church we attend; it may be a warm hug, a pat on the back, a kiss on the cheek, a friendly shake of the hand; it could be any of those, for the method is not that important, the motive certainly is. Surely one of the best ways to show others our love is through the acceptance we whisper to them, together with a warm touch. To me, the all-important truth to emerge from this Pauline suggestion is that we treat our fellow pilgrims not only with courtesy, but also with affection according to the conventions of our own culture.

5:27

For public consumption

Paul gives another one of those directives for which he is famous when he says, *I put you under oath before the Lord to have this letter read to all the brothers.* He pulls no punches when he says that he wants his letter to be read out in public before the whole congregation. It is not to be read only to a handful of committee folk gathered in a back room or tucked away in a discreet corner at the rear of a building. His epistle is addressed to the entire church family; there is something in it for each of them and there is so much in it for all of them!

5:28

Grace for the journey

Finally, he writes, *The grace of our Lord Jesus Christ be with you*. What an extraordinarily great benediction! At the start of the letter, Paul said to them, 'Hello, grace to you.' Now, at the end of the letter, he writes, 'Cheerio, grace be with you.'

The life-changing grace of God saves us. It sustains us and never fails to strengthen us. It does not matter what type of situation we find ourselves in, God's grace is sufficient in that it is immeasurable. We become fruitful by grace; we persevere by grace; we mature by grace. When we think of God's amazing grace, we think of something truly undeserved. Always unearned. And always unrepayable. Here is the scandal of free grace.

Why grace? Charles Swindoll in *The Grace Awakening* says, 'What is it that frees us to be all he means us to be? Grace. What is it that permits others to be who they are, even very different from us? Grace. What allows us to disagree, yet stimulates us to press on? Grace. What adds oil to the friction points of a marriage, freeing both partners from pettiness and negativism? Grace. And what gives magnetic charm to a ministry, inviting others to become a part? Again, it is grace.'

Paul knew their surroundings, he is familiar with their situation, he is conscious of their problems and difficulties, he is all too aware of their changing circumstances. And so, the preacher man warmly commends them to the grace of God and to the one who is the God of all grace.

A concluding reference to grace was almost always his signature tune, so central was it to his whole theology. It is no empty, conventional formula, for grace is the heart of the gospel and the heart of God. Pass it on – grace!

The frisson of faith

Well, believe it or not, we have come to the end of the book, but the good news is, we have not come to the end of the grace of God, for the grace of God is lasting and limitless. There is always more to come, and then some! The Puritan Richard Sibbes (1577-1635) in his book, *The Tender Heart*, reminds us that 'God crowns grace with grace.' God says to each of us right now, 'My grace is there for you. It is *with you,* make the most of it.'

When we do, our passion for the Lord will be contagious, and to crown it all, there will be a heady air of expectation in our relationship with the Saviour. Burning hearts. Fast-beating hearts. Nothing but hope and the grace of God can accomplish this! And that, praise God, is where gospel people, gospel grace, and gospel churches excel.